I0474394

Real World
Colouring Book
For Advanced Users & Adults

50 Images

**Created From Real Life Photos
For You To Colour As You Please.**

ISBN 978-0-359-93585-7
90000
9 780359 935857

HANSON

KEEP
RIVEWAY
CLEAR

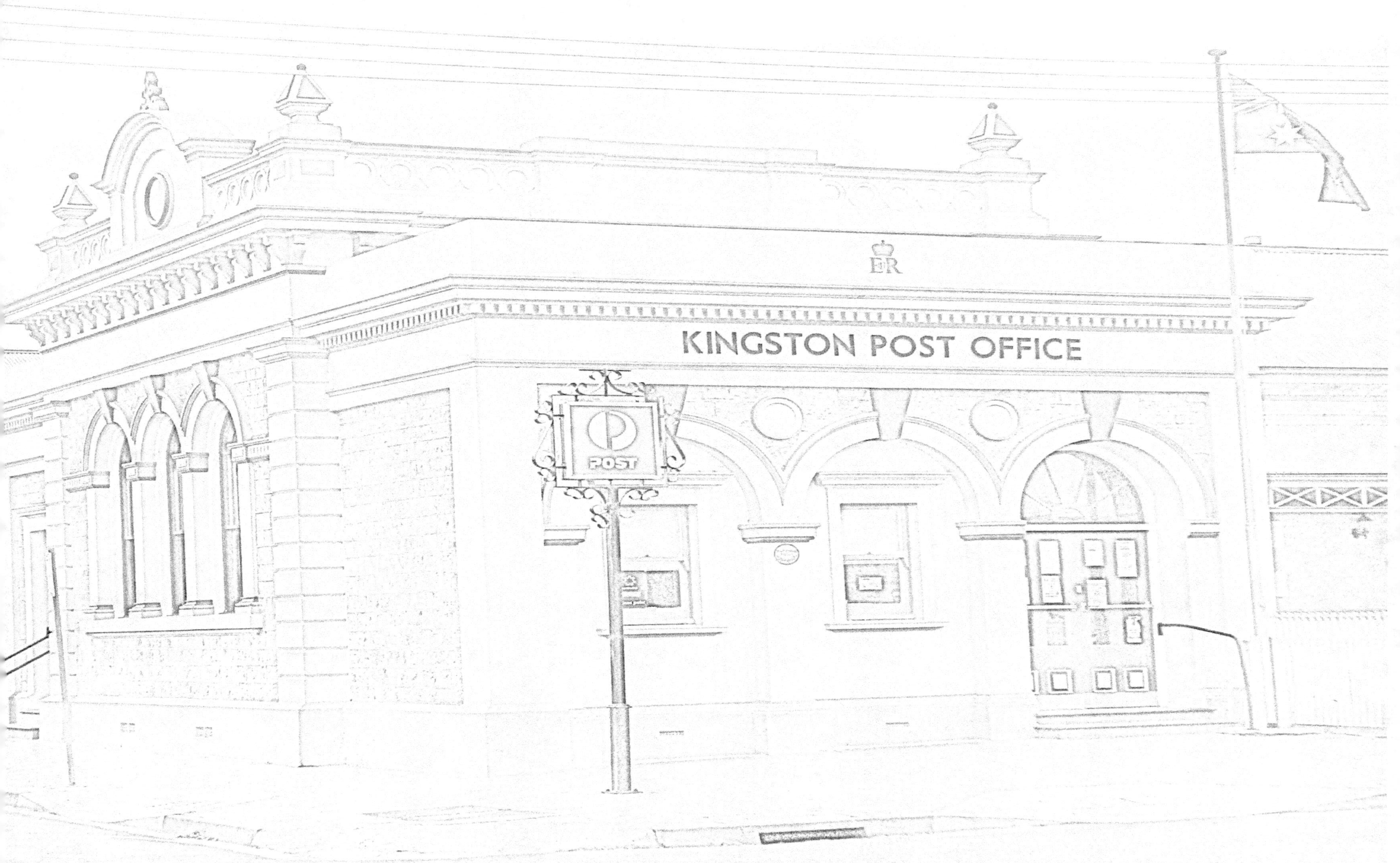
ER
KINGSTON POST OFFICE
POST

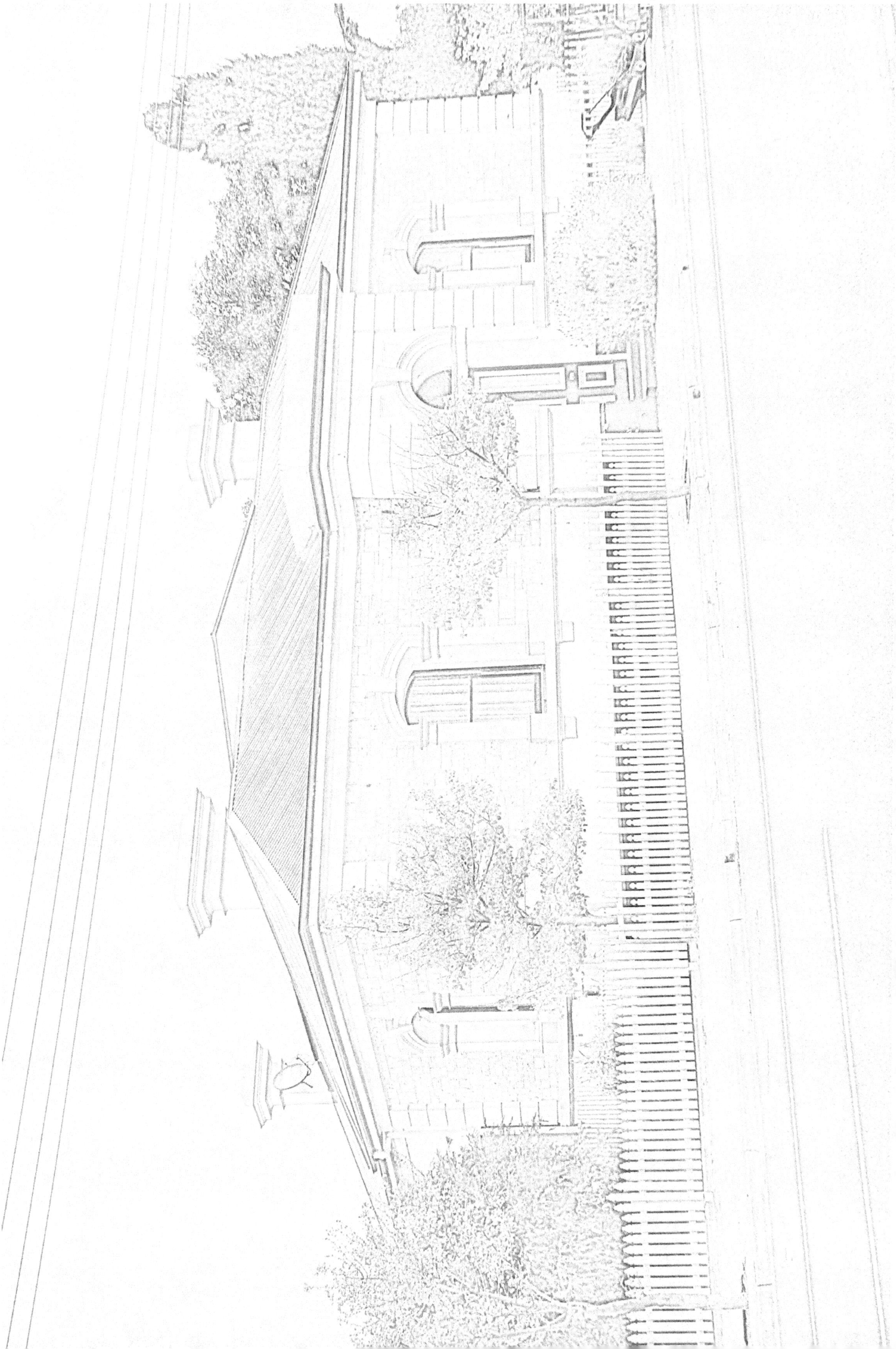

IRRIGATION OFFICE

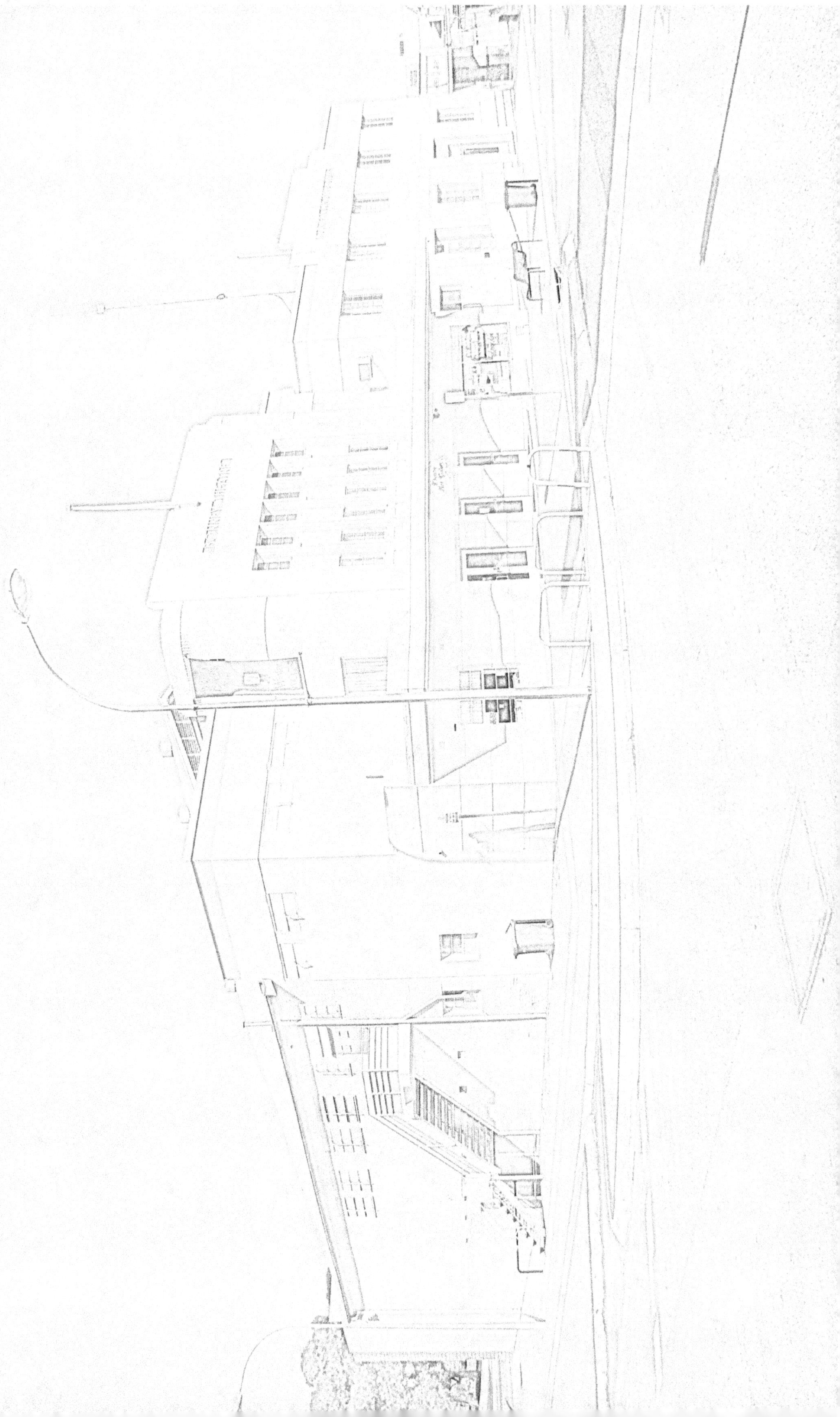

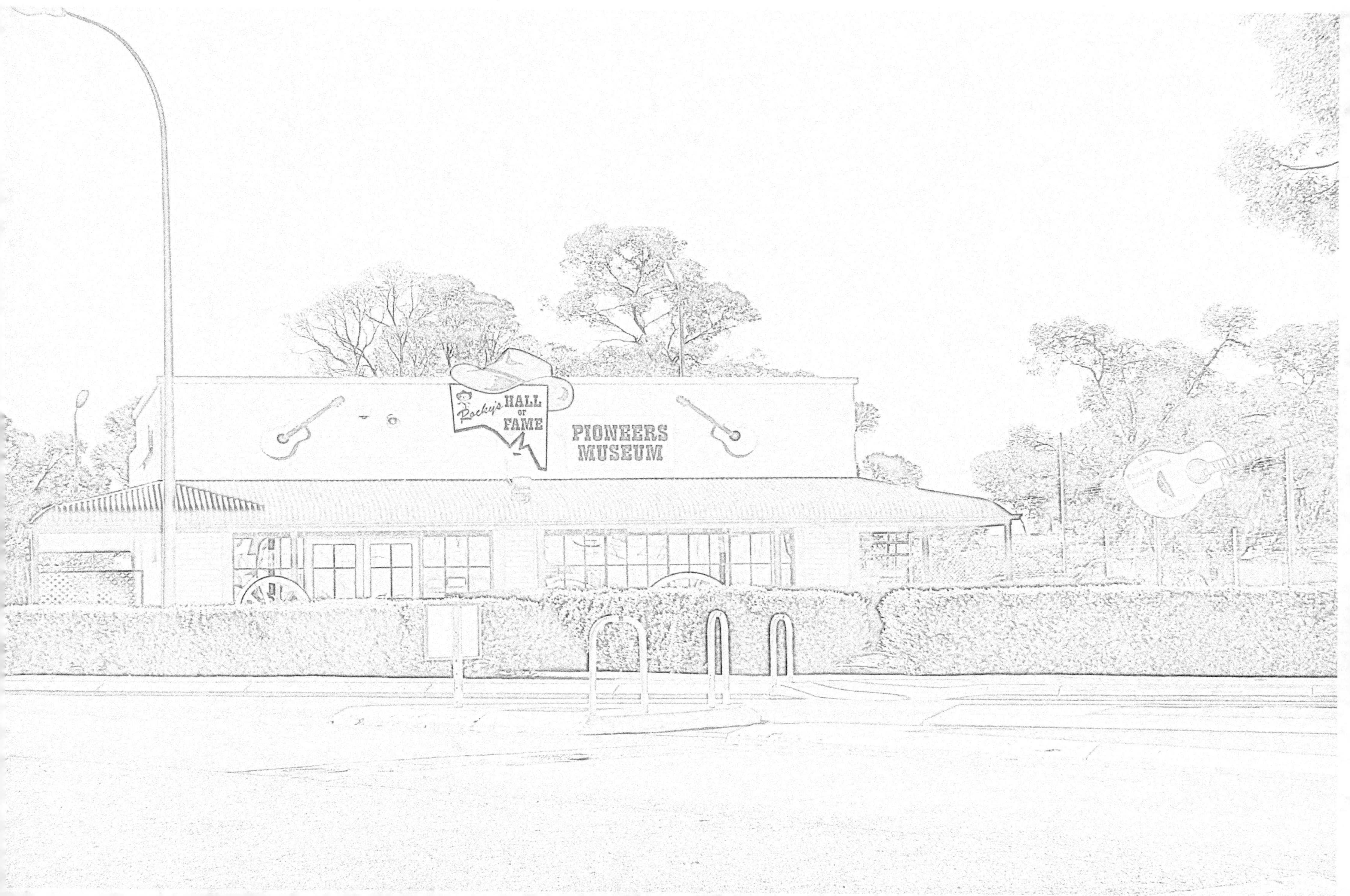
Rocky's HALL OF FAME
PIONEERS MUSEUM

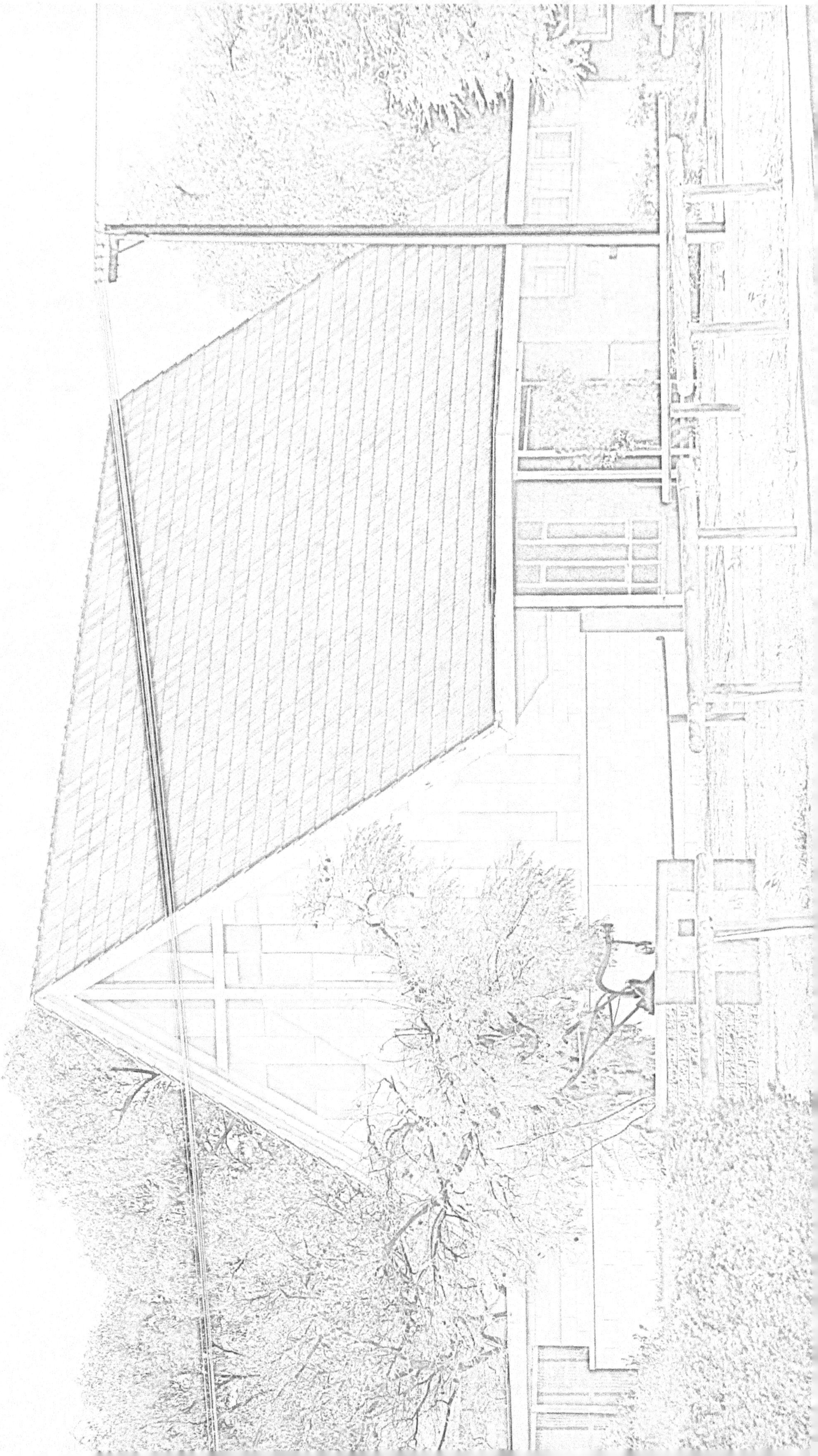

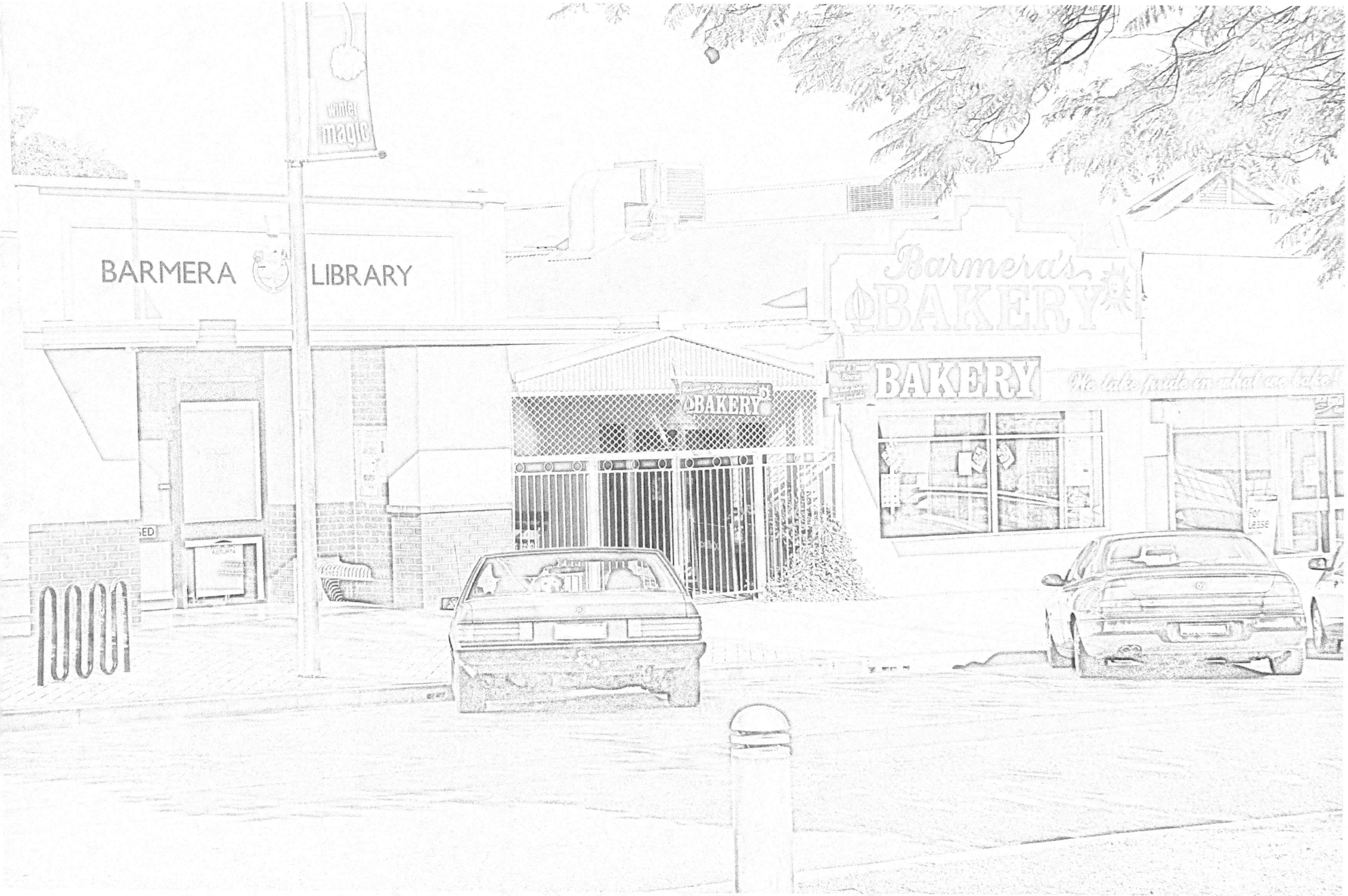
winter
magic
BARMERA LIBRARY
Barmera's
BAKERY
BAKERY
BAKERY
For Lease

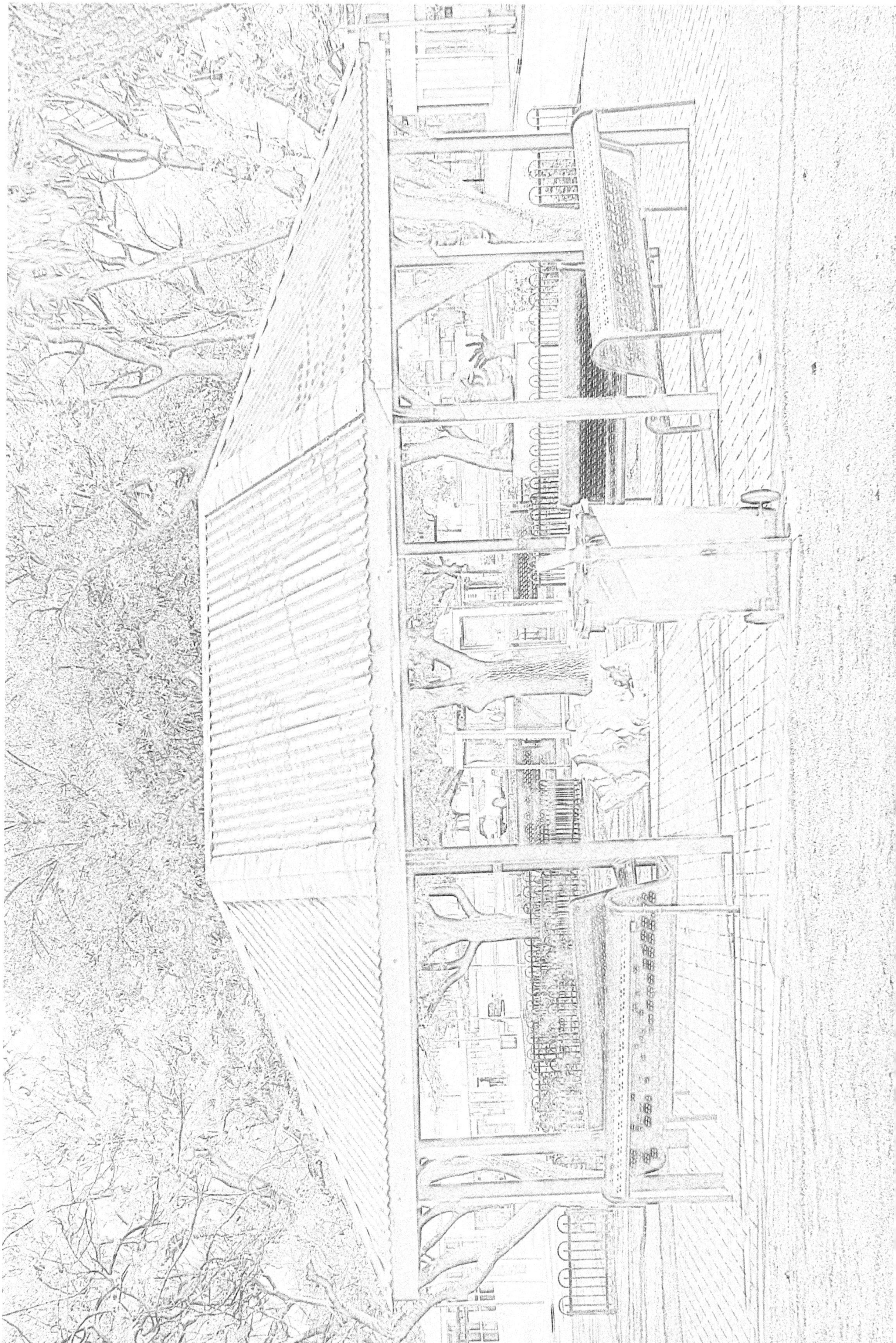

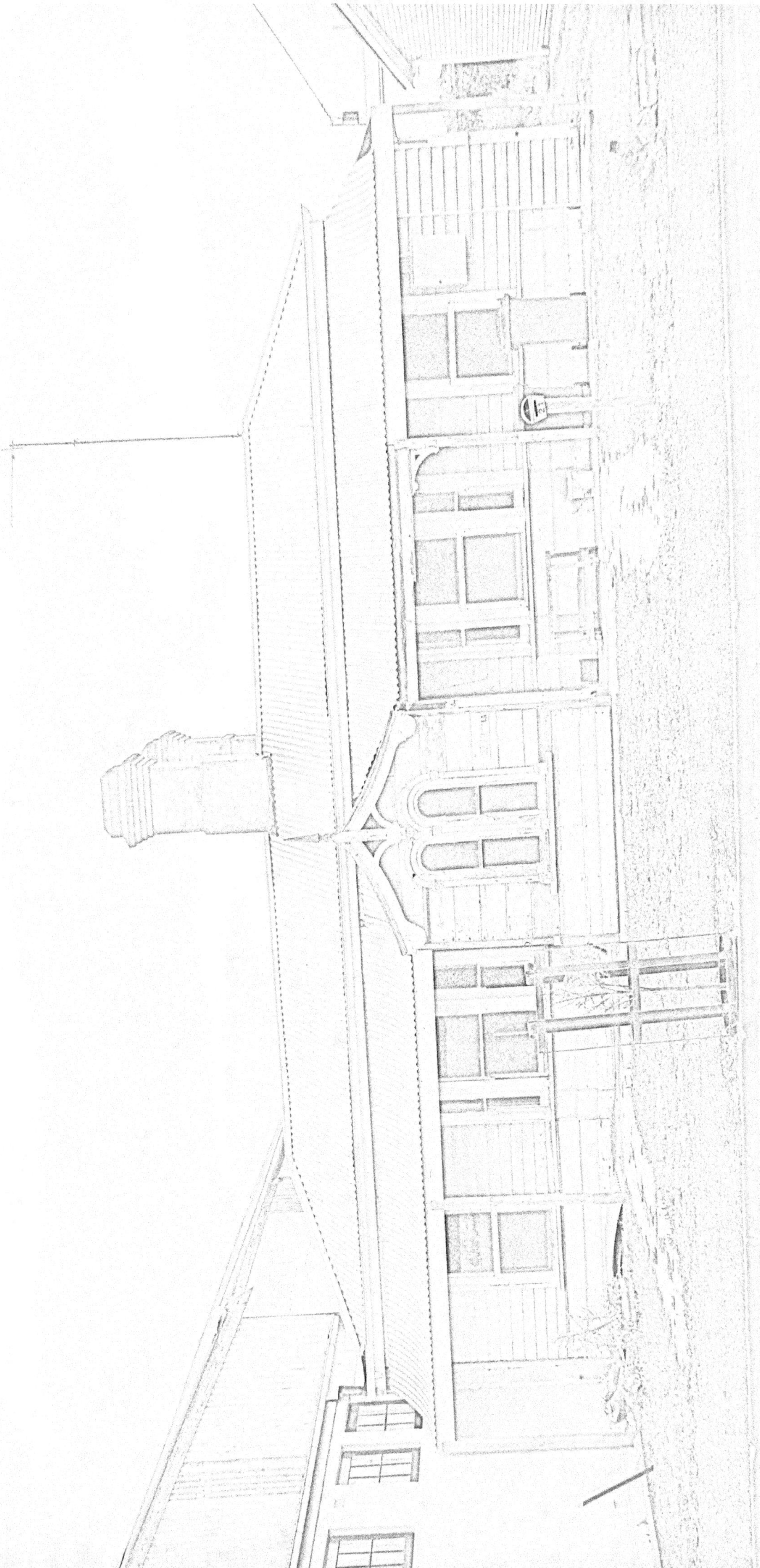

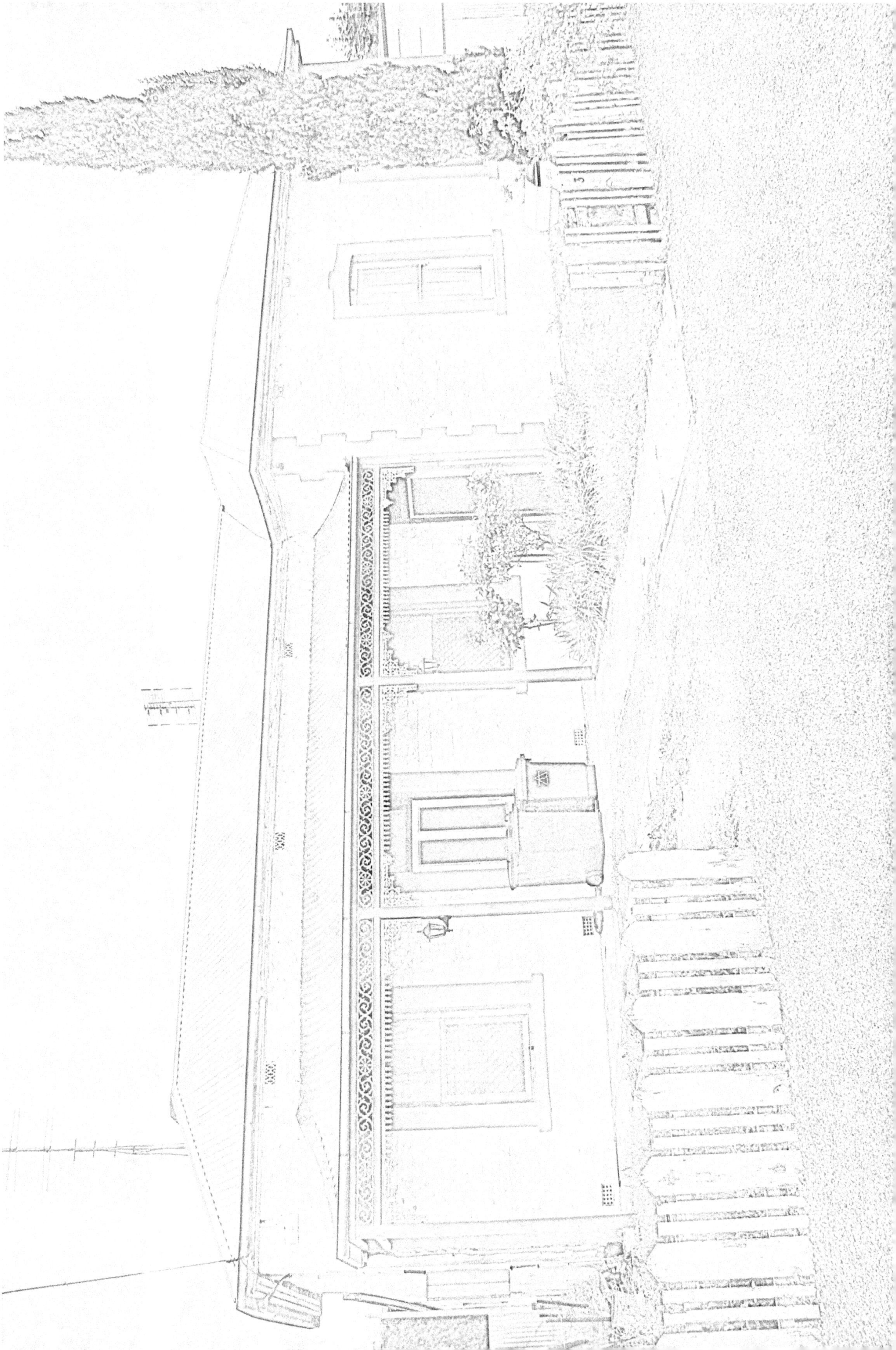

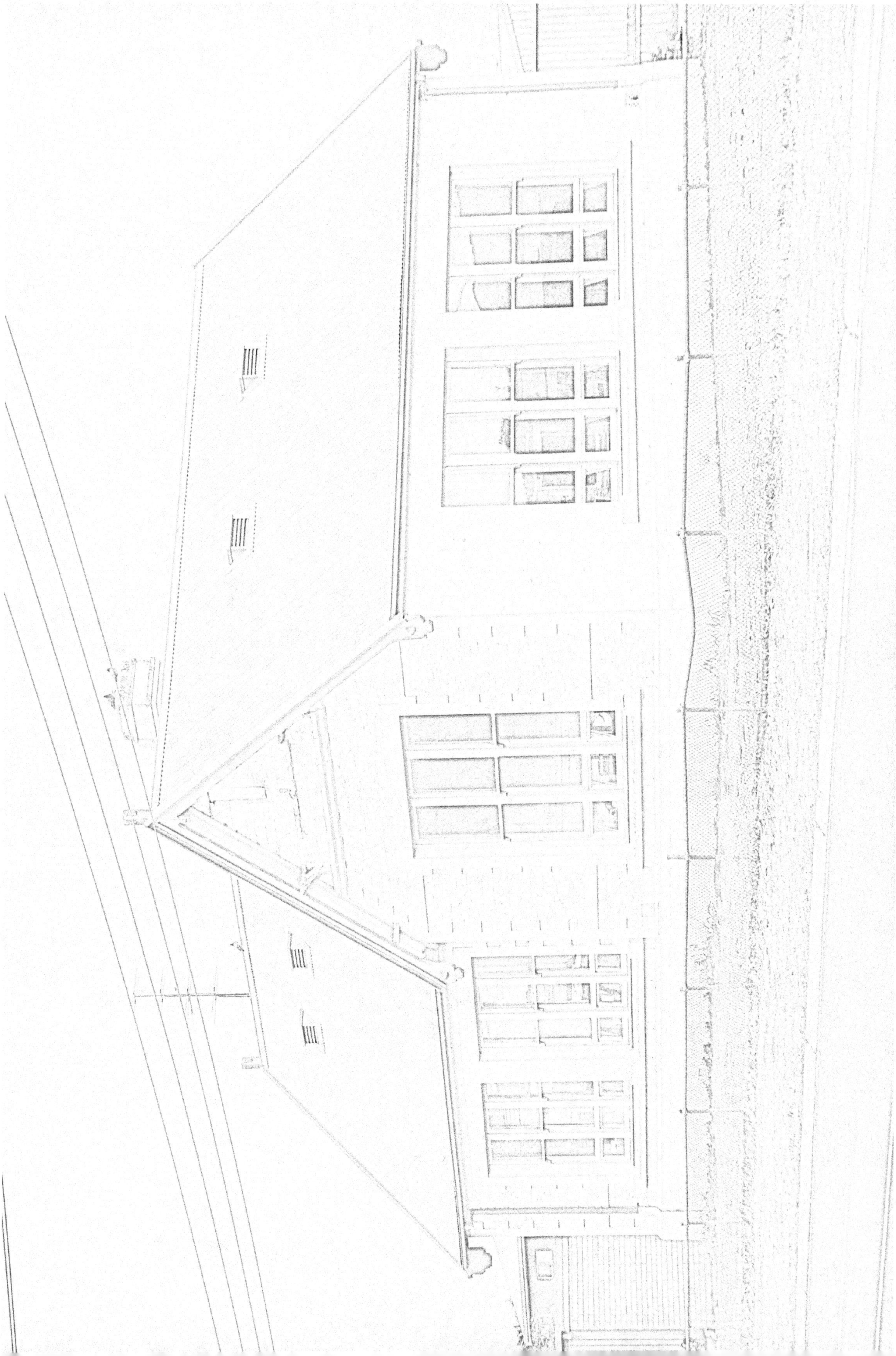

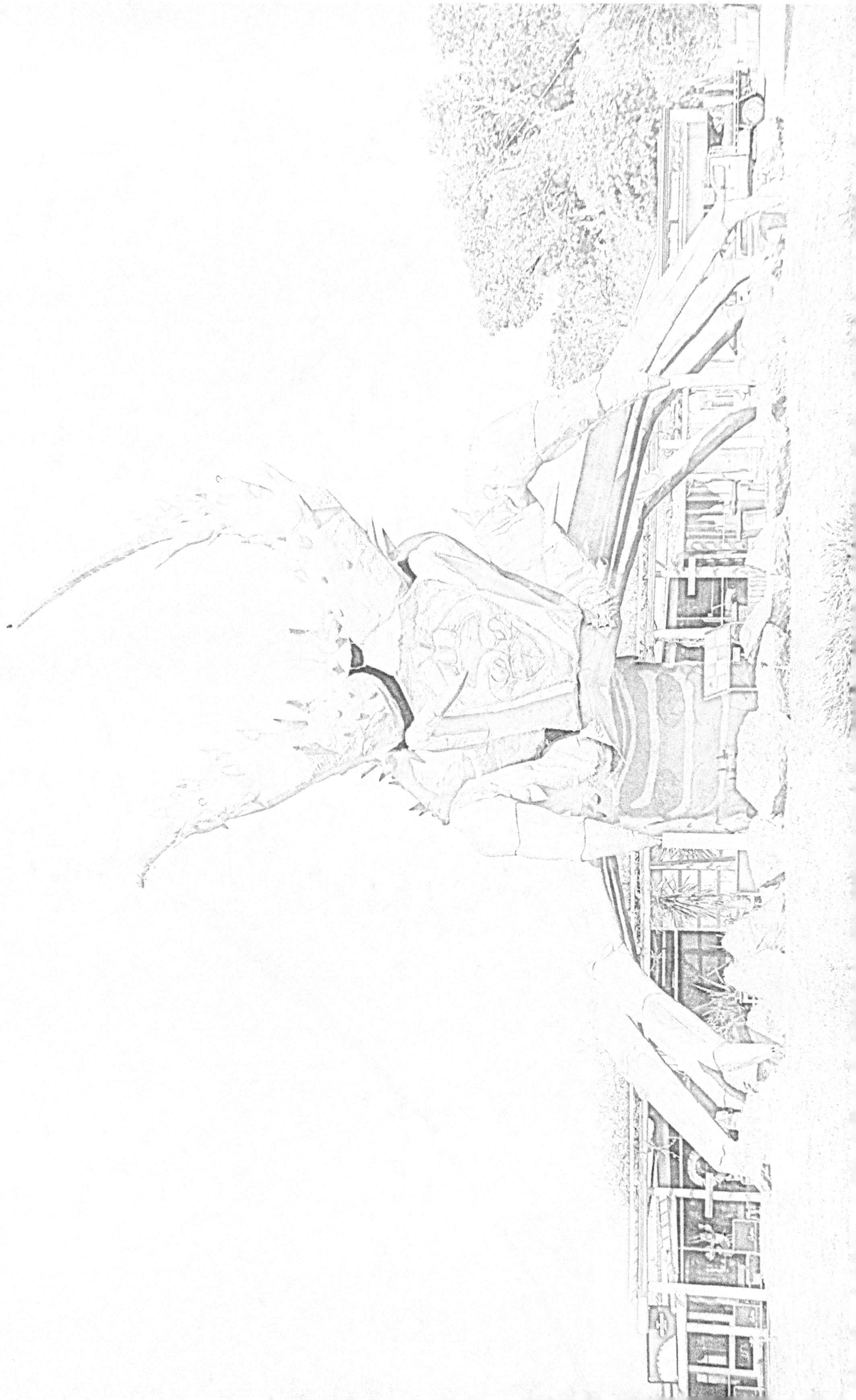

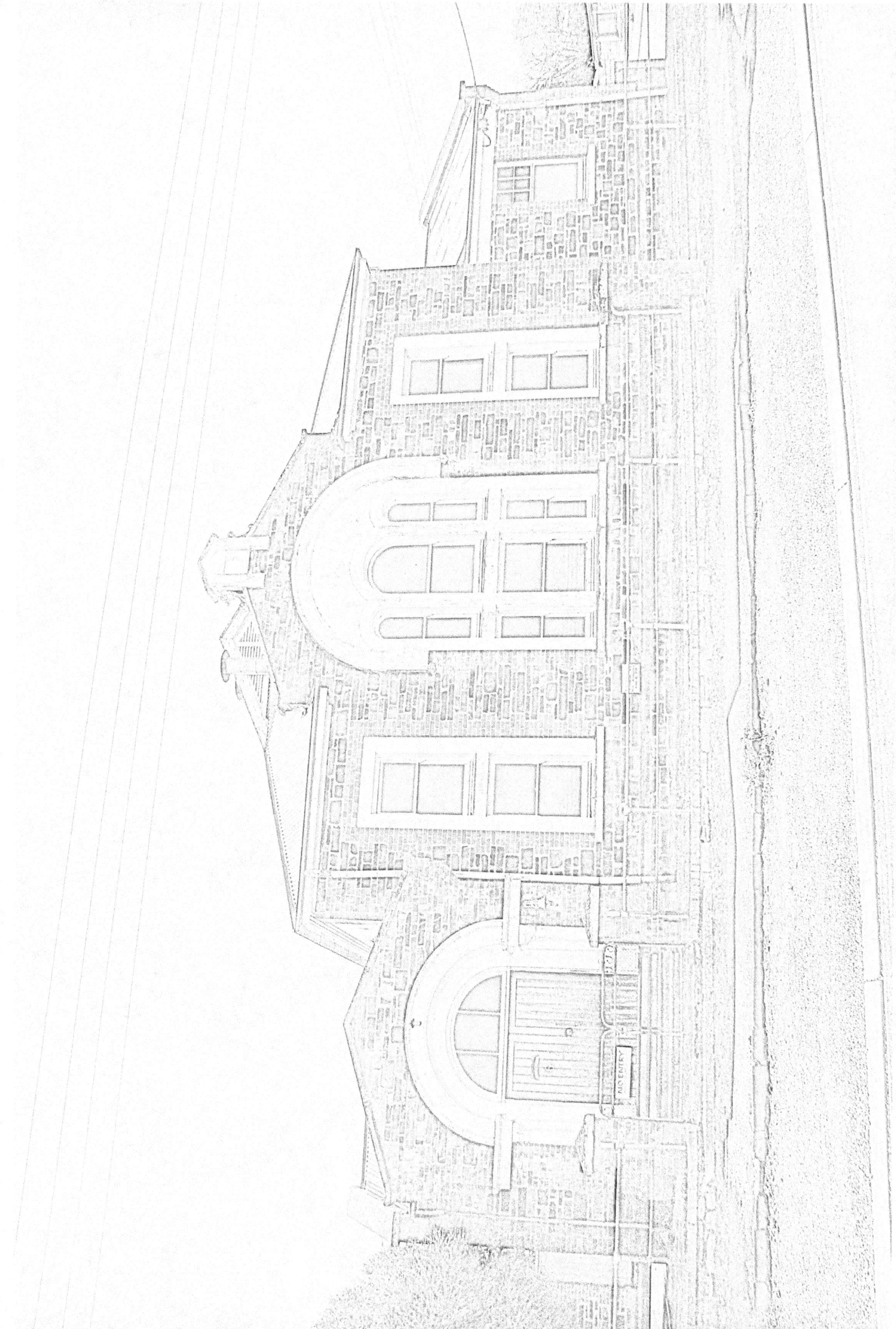

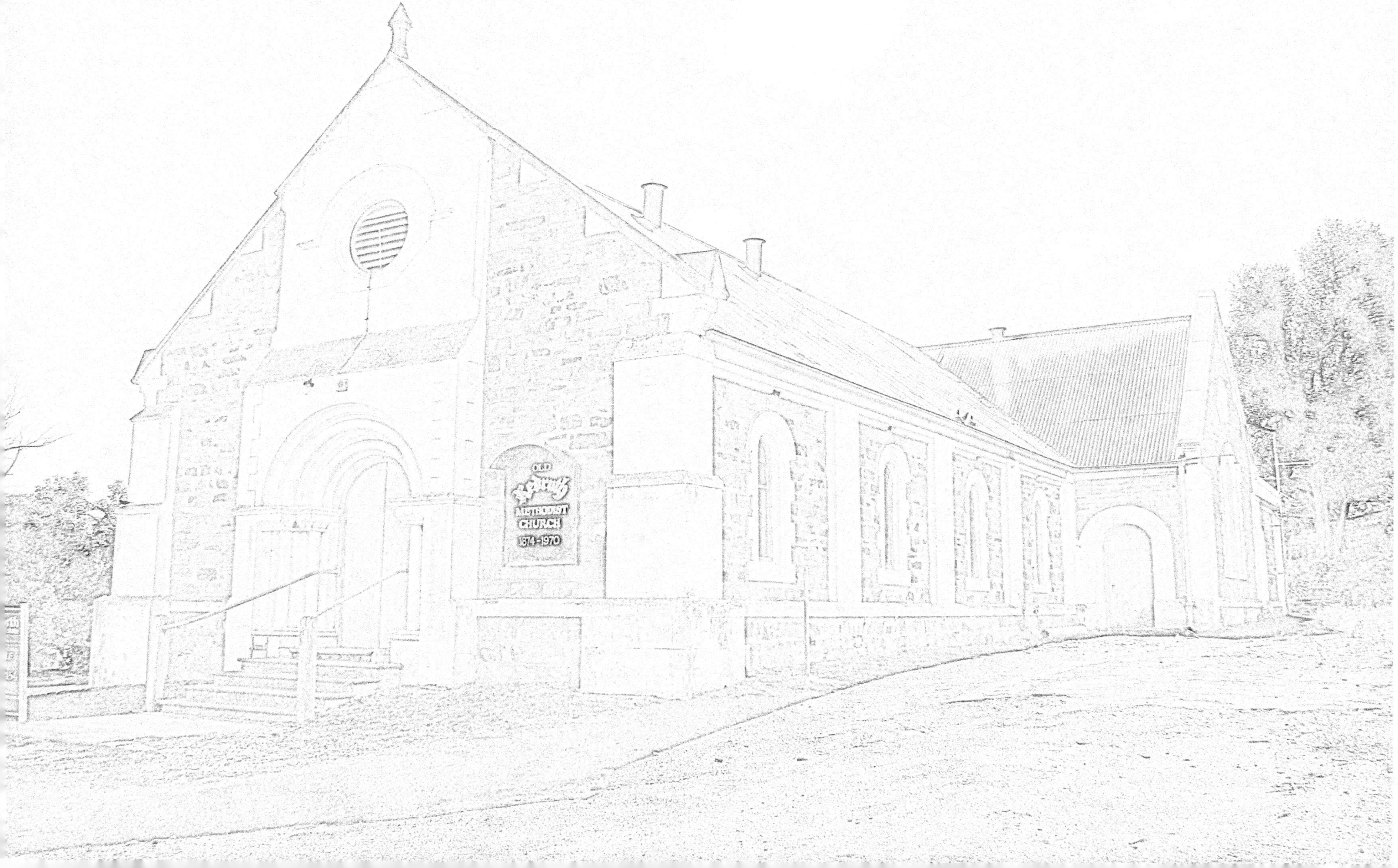
OLD
METHODIST
CHURCH
1874-1970

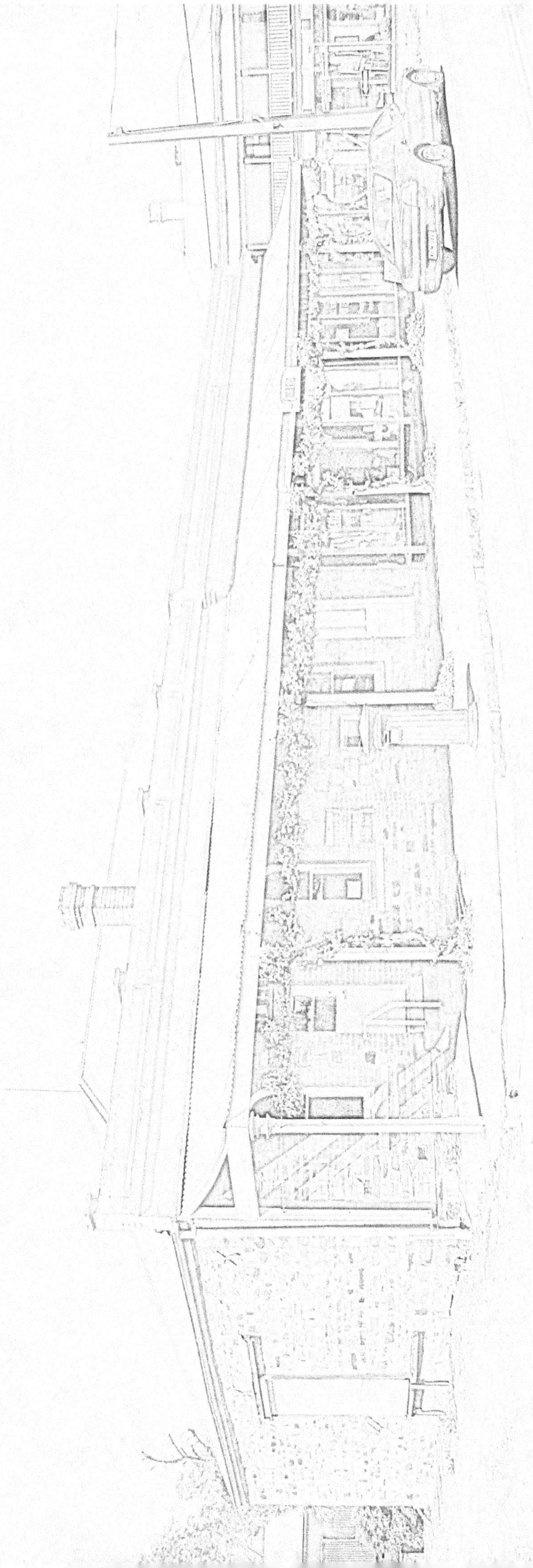

FOSTER'S
LAGER
WEST
END
HOTEL
BURRA
HERITAGE TRAIL
16
Takeaway
Open 7 Days
POKIES
MEALS
GUINNESS
ATM

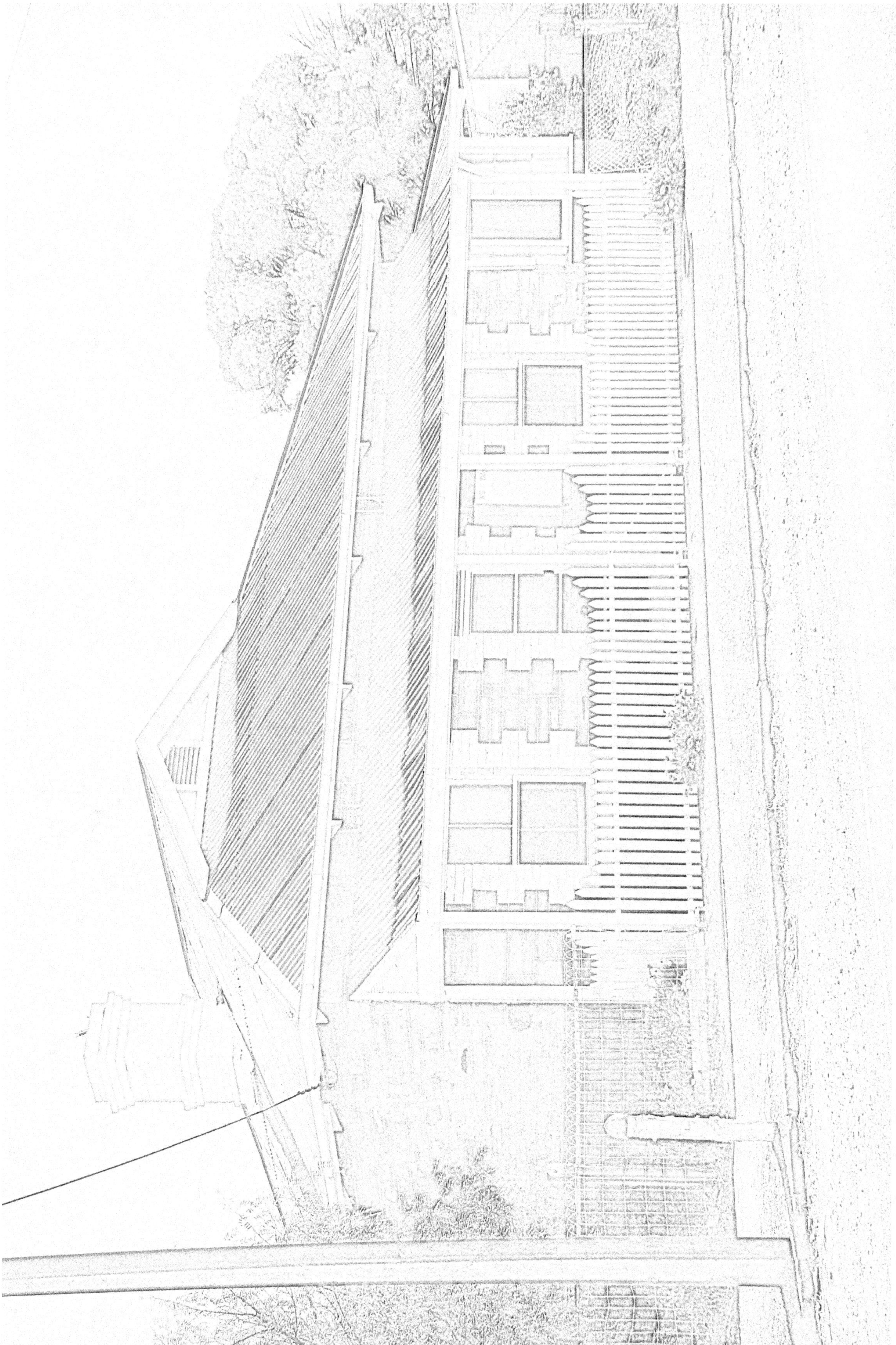

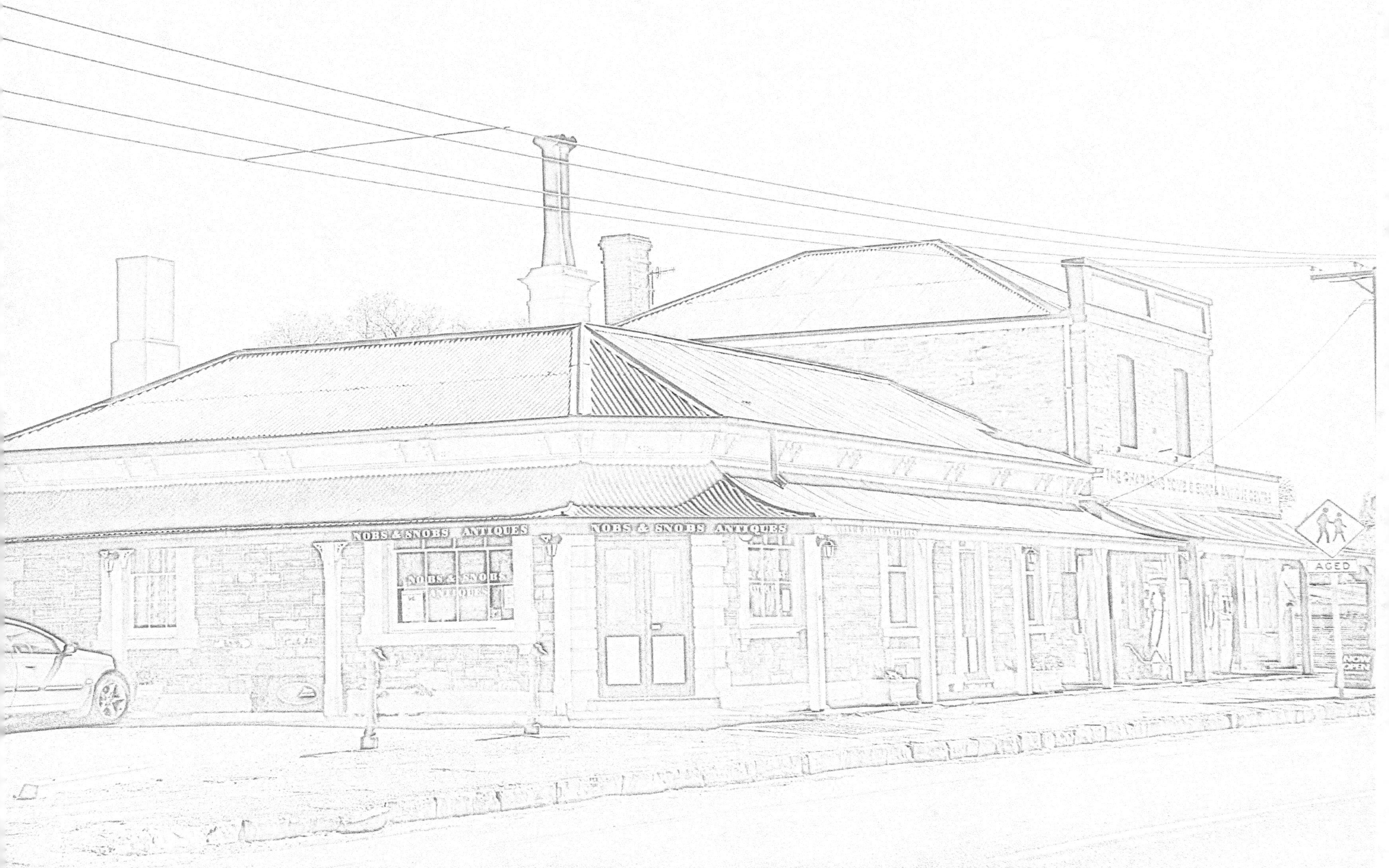
NOBS & SNOBS ANTIQUES
NOBS & SNOBS ANTIQUES
NOBS & SNOBS
ANTIQUES
AGED

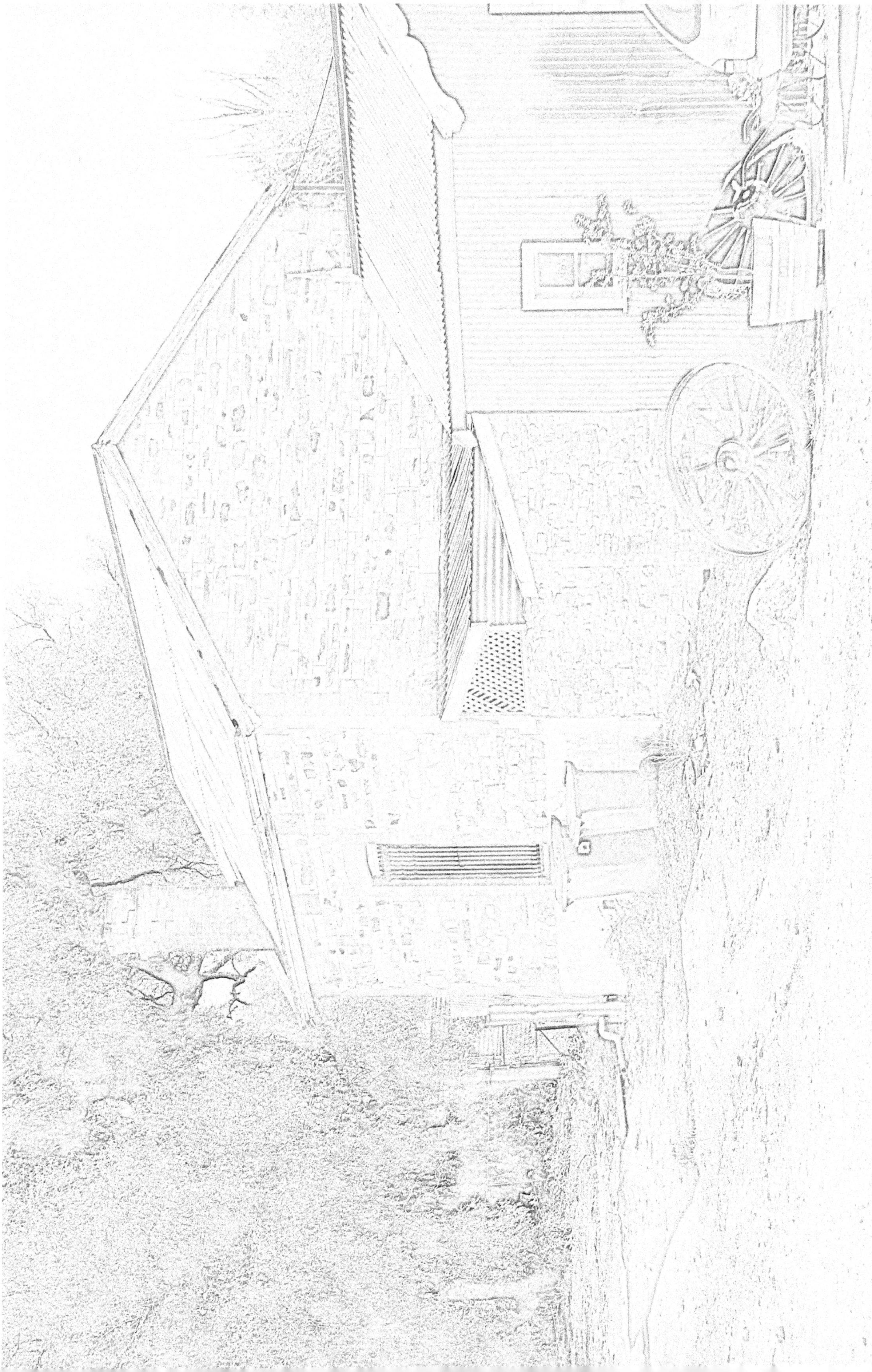

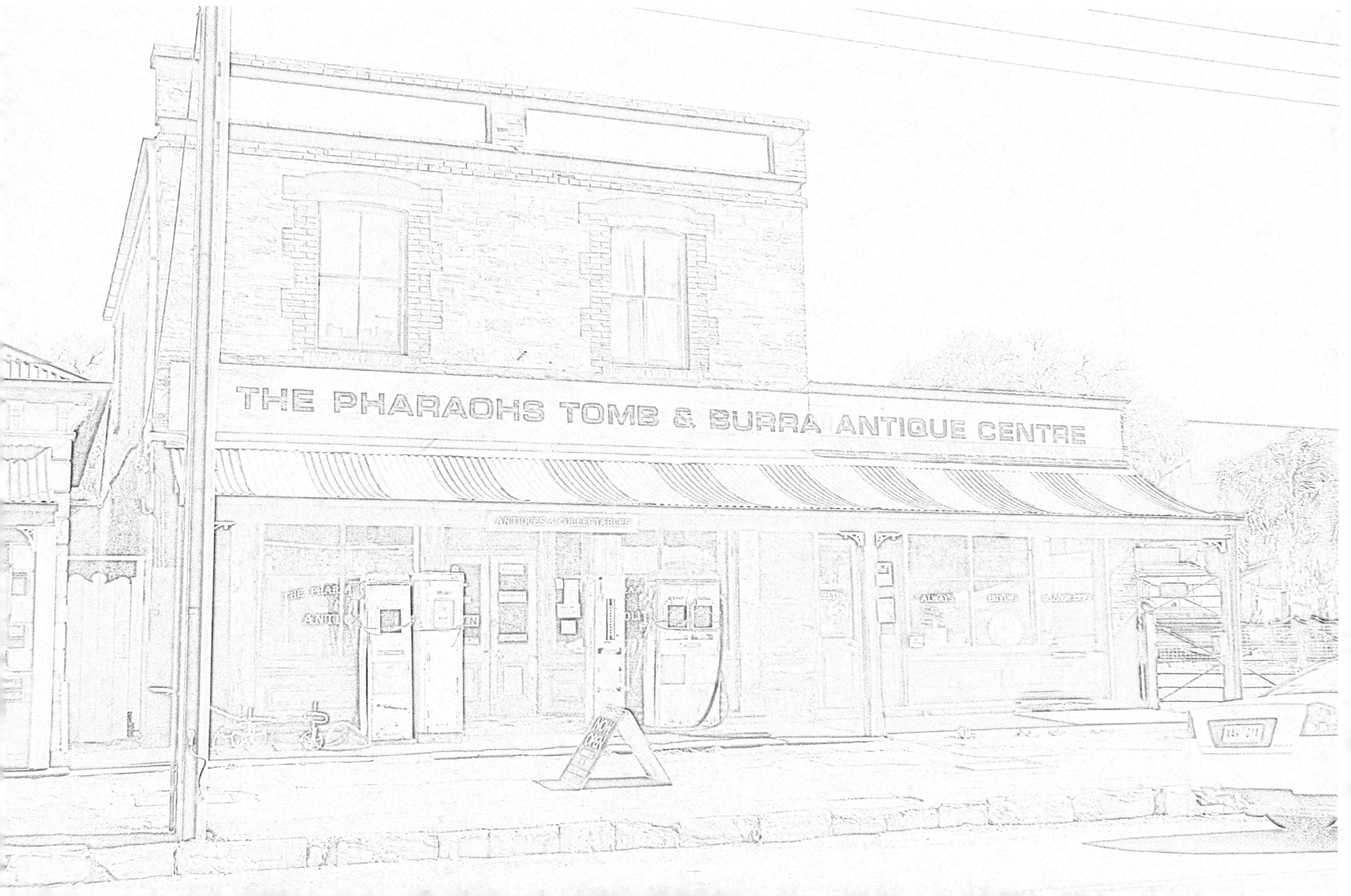
THE PHARAOHS TOMB & BURRA ANTIQUE CENTRE
ANTIQUES & COLLECTABLES
ALWAYS
BUYING

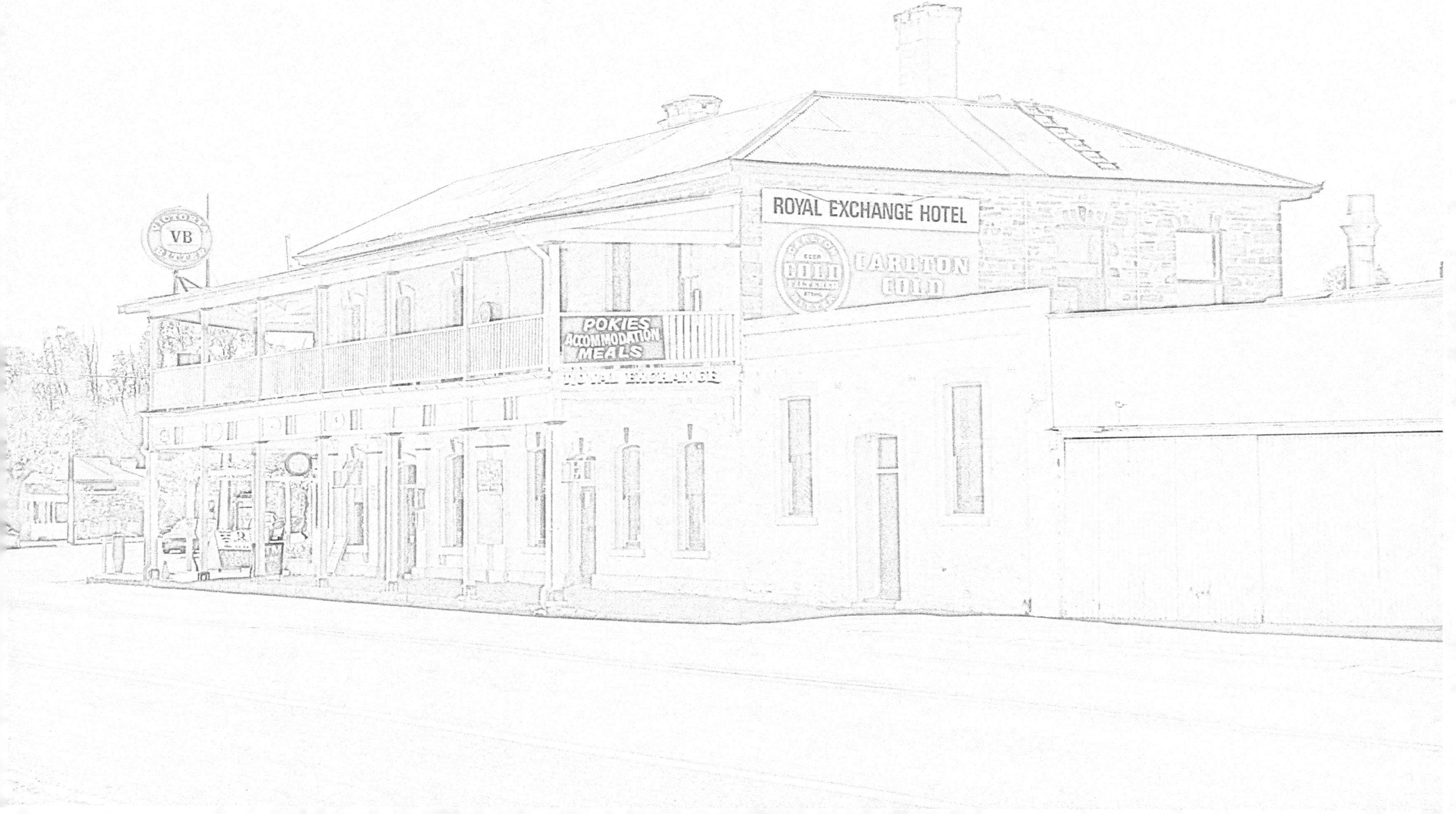
ROYAL EXCHANGE HOTEL
CARLTON COLD
POKIES
ACCOMMODATION
MEALS
ROYAL EXCHANGE
VB

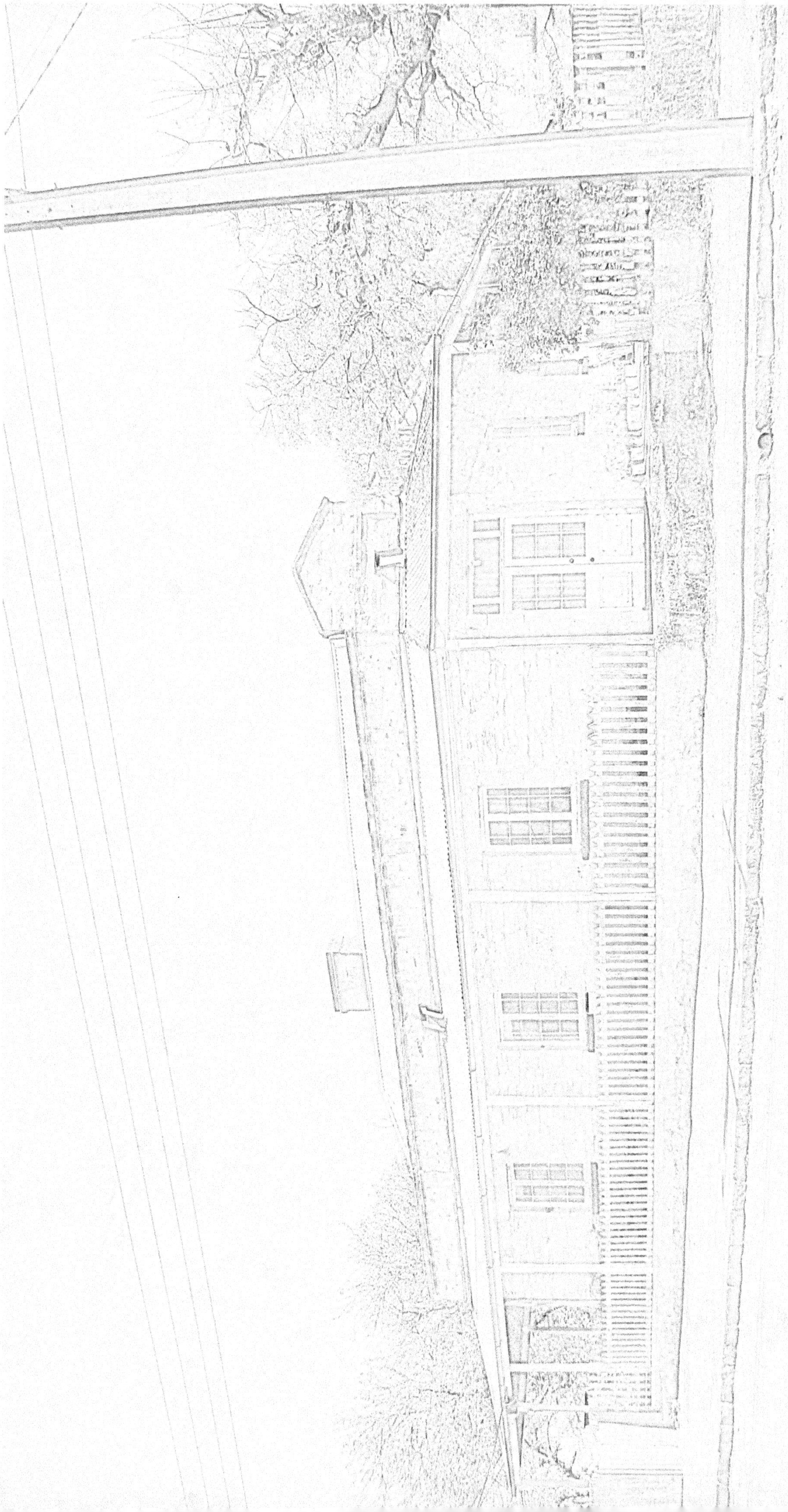

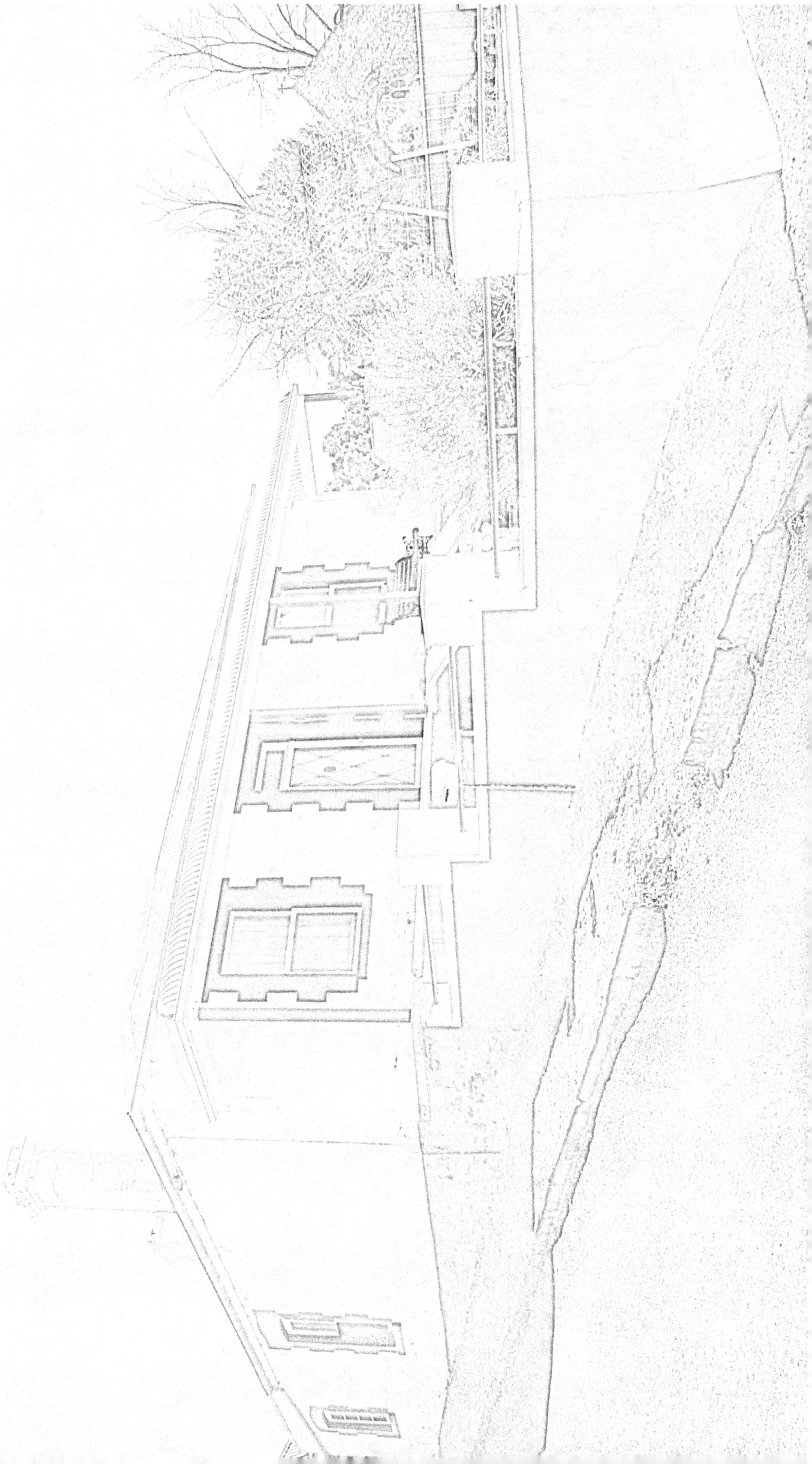

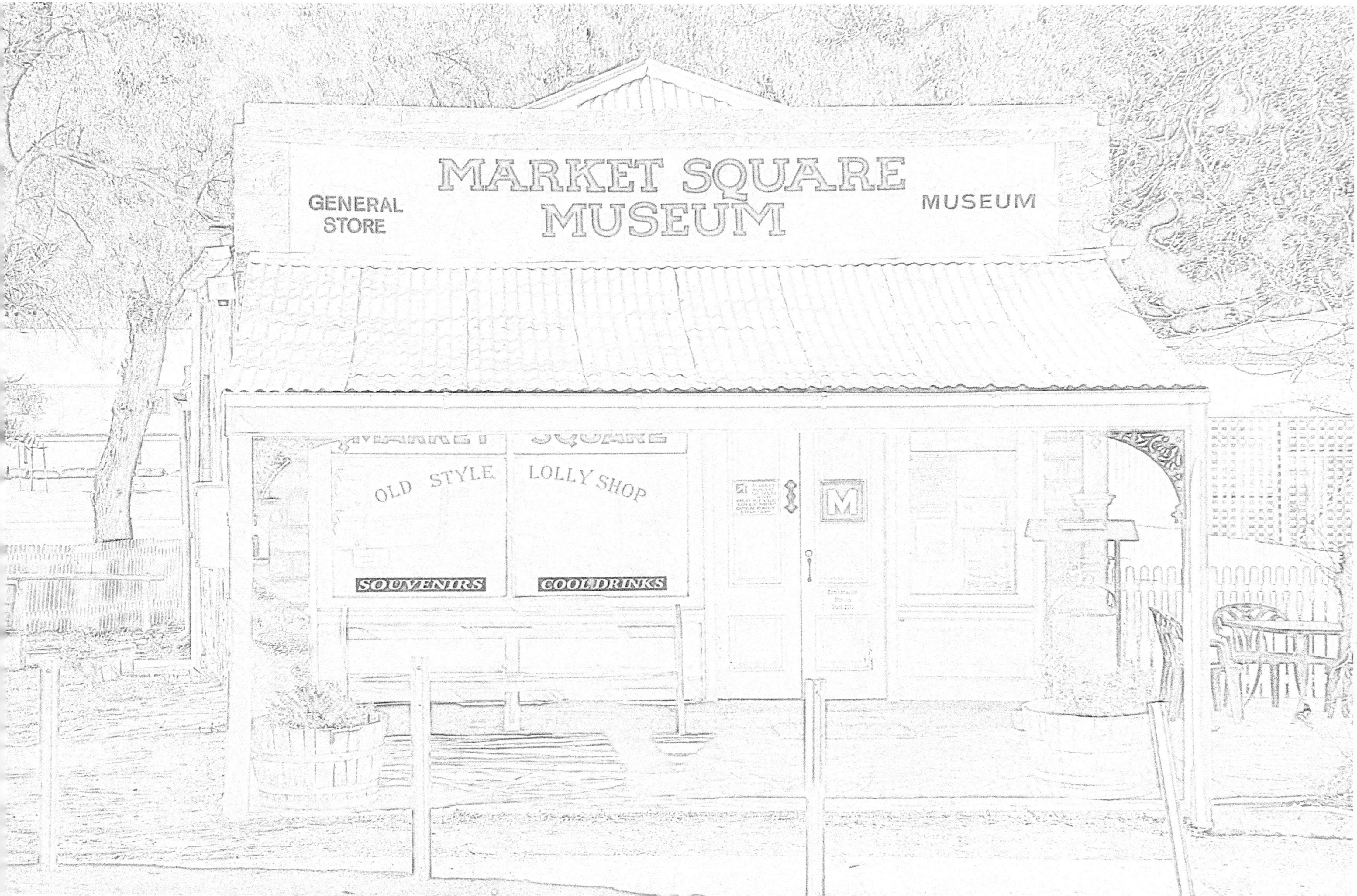
GENERAL
STORE
MARKET SQUARE
MUSEUM
MUSEUM
OLD STYLE
LOLLY SHOP
SOUVENIRS
COOLDRINKS
M

NEW MARKET
ADELAIDE EXCHANGE
FRUIT & COMPANY
PRODUCE LIMITED
EROS
ΚΑΦΕ
NO ENTRY

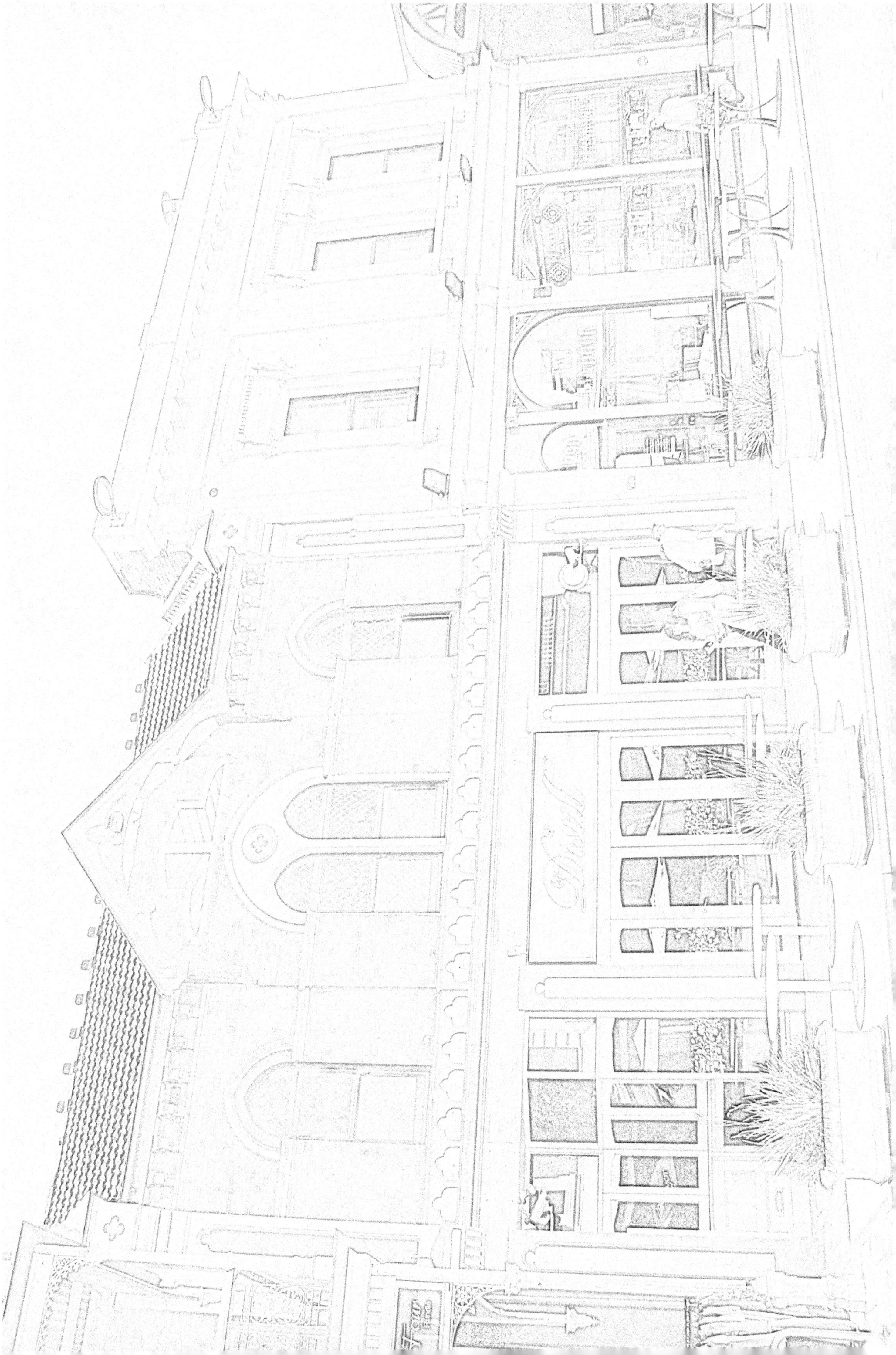

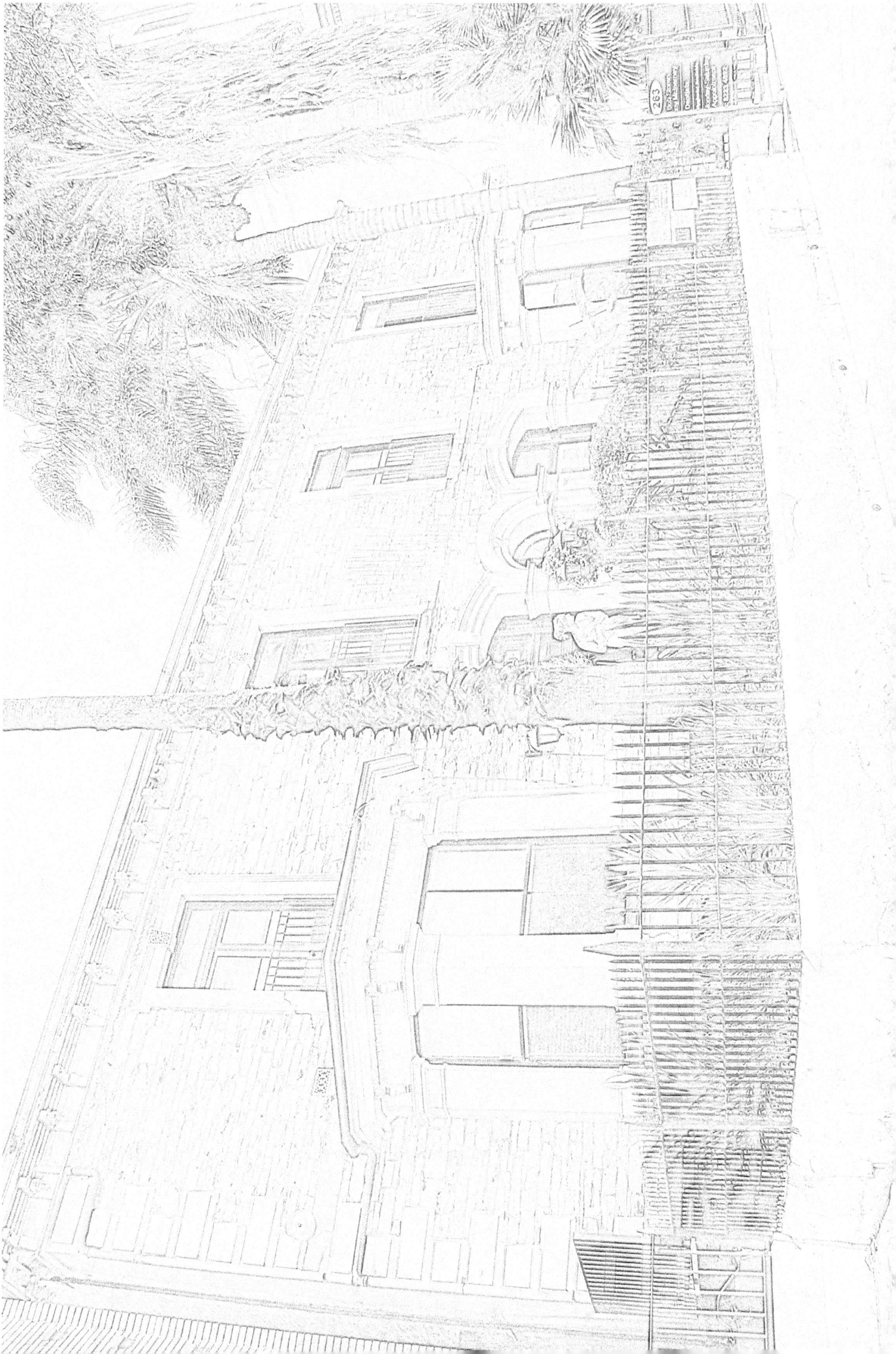
263

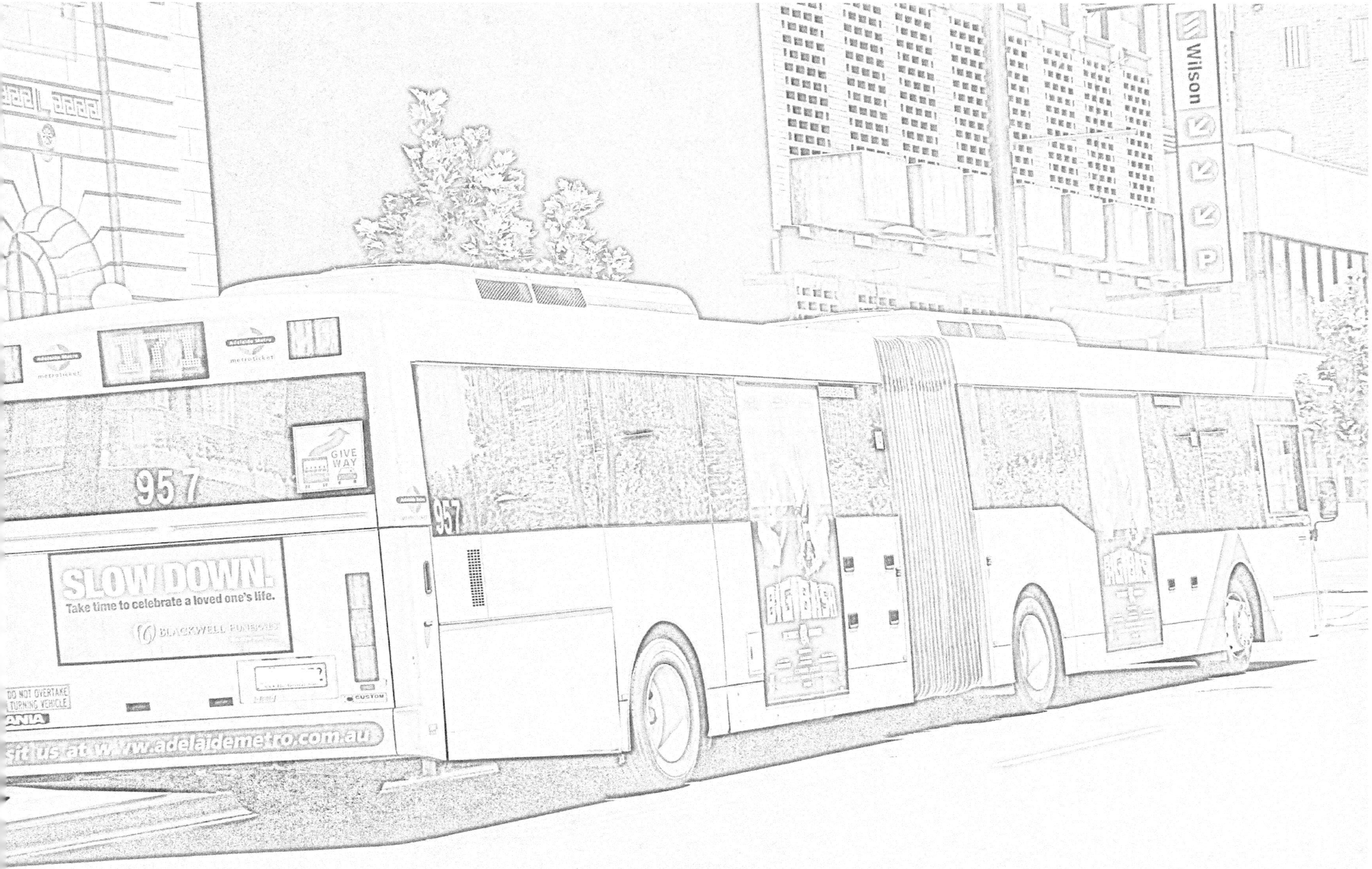
Wilson
P
957
GIVE WAY
957
SLOW DOWN.
Take time to celebrate a loved one's life.
BLACKWELL
DO NOT OVERTAKE TURNING VEHICLE
CUSTOM
sit us at www.adelaidemetro.com.au
BIG BASH

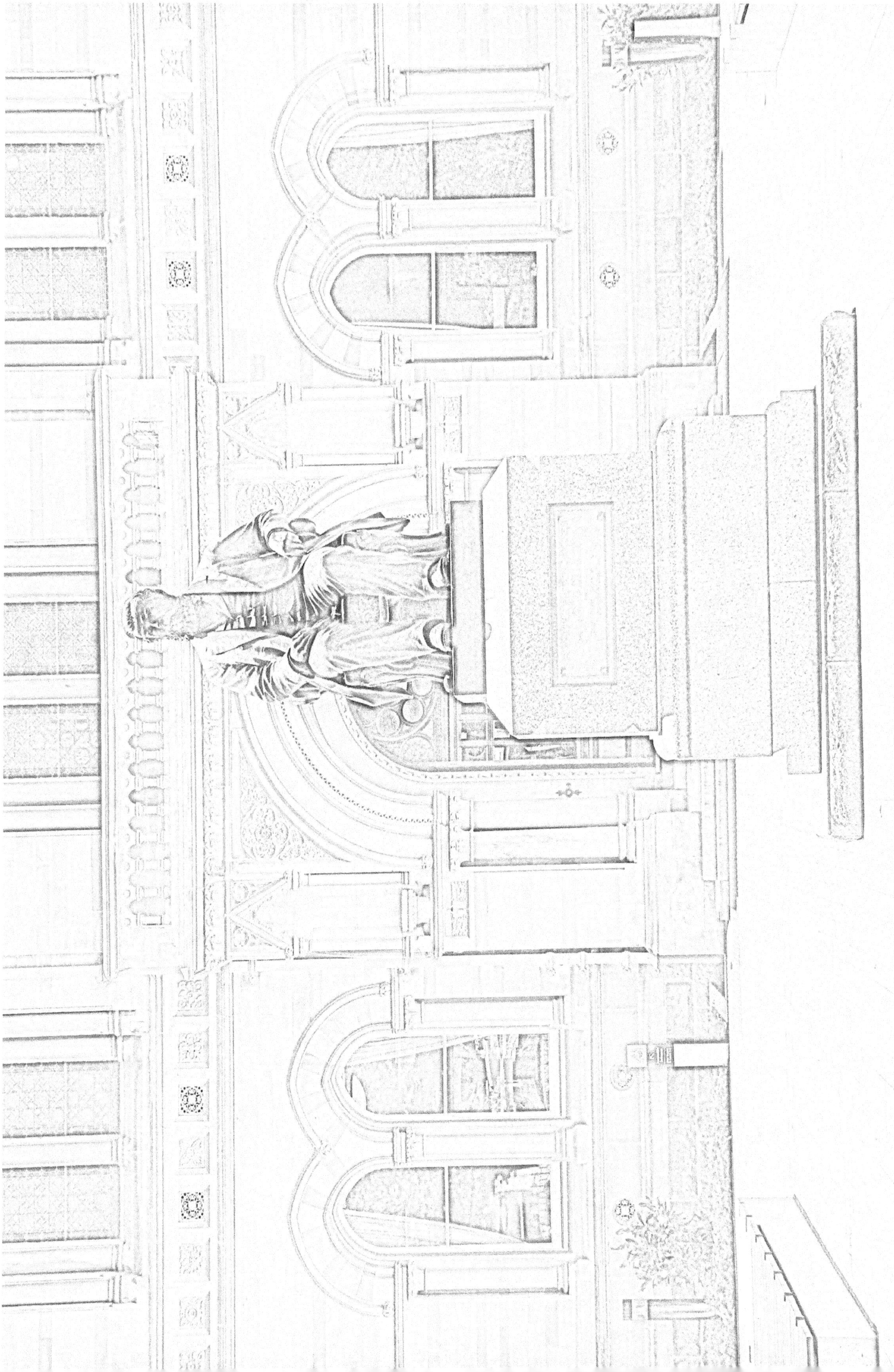

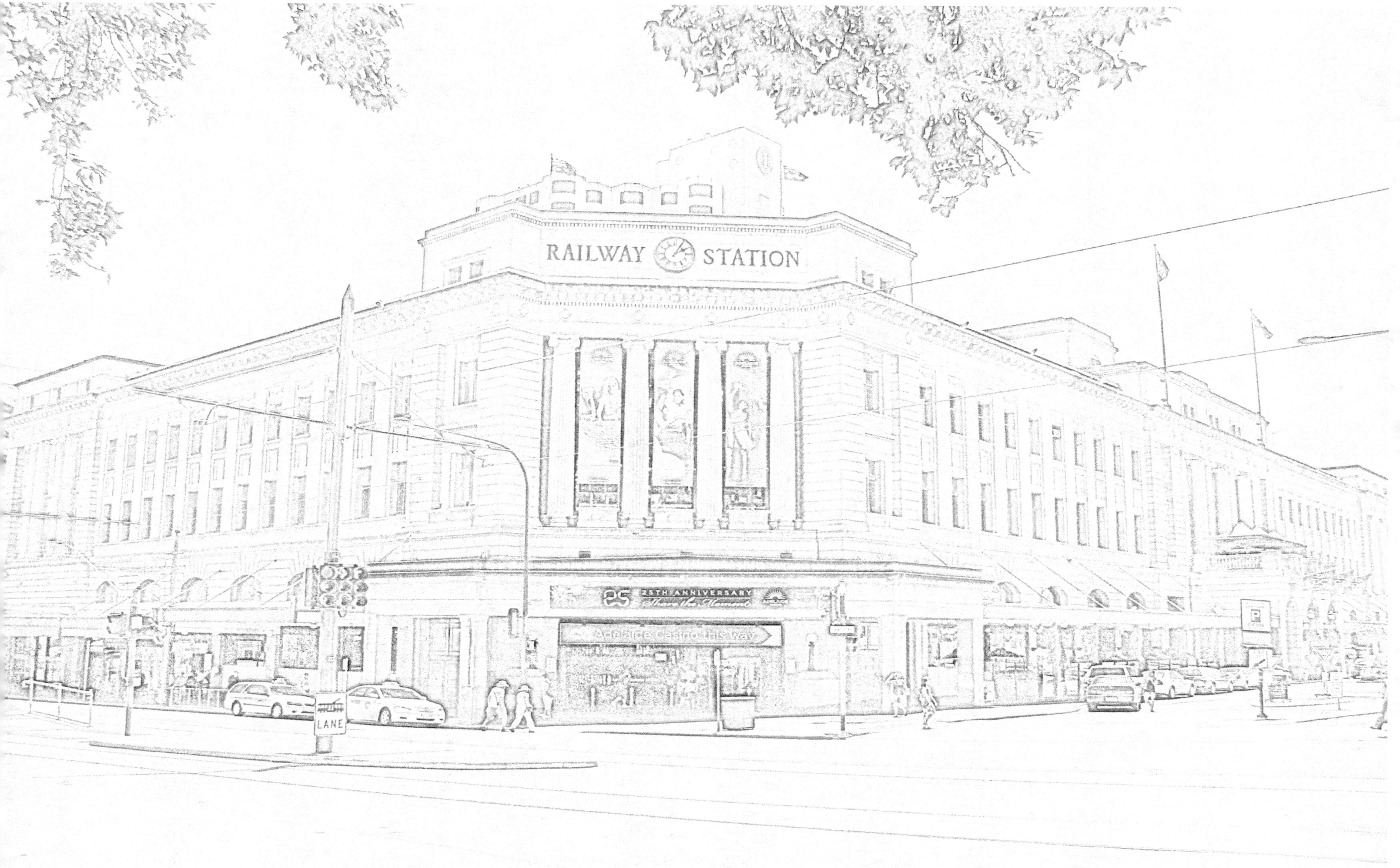
RAILWAY STATION
25 25TH ANNIVERSARY
Adelaide Casino this way
LANE

LANE

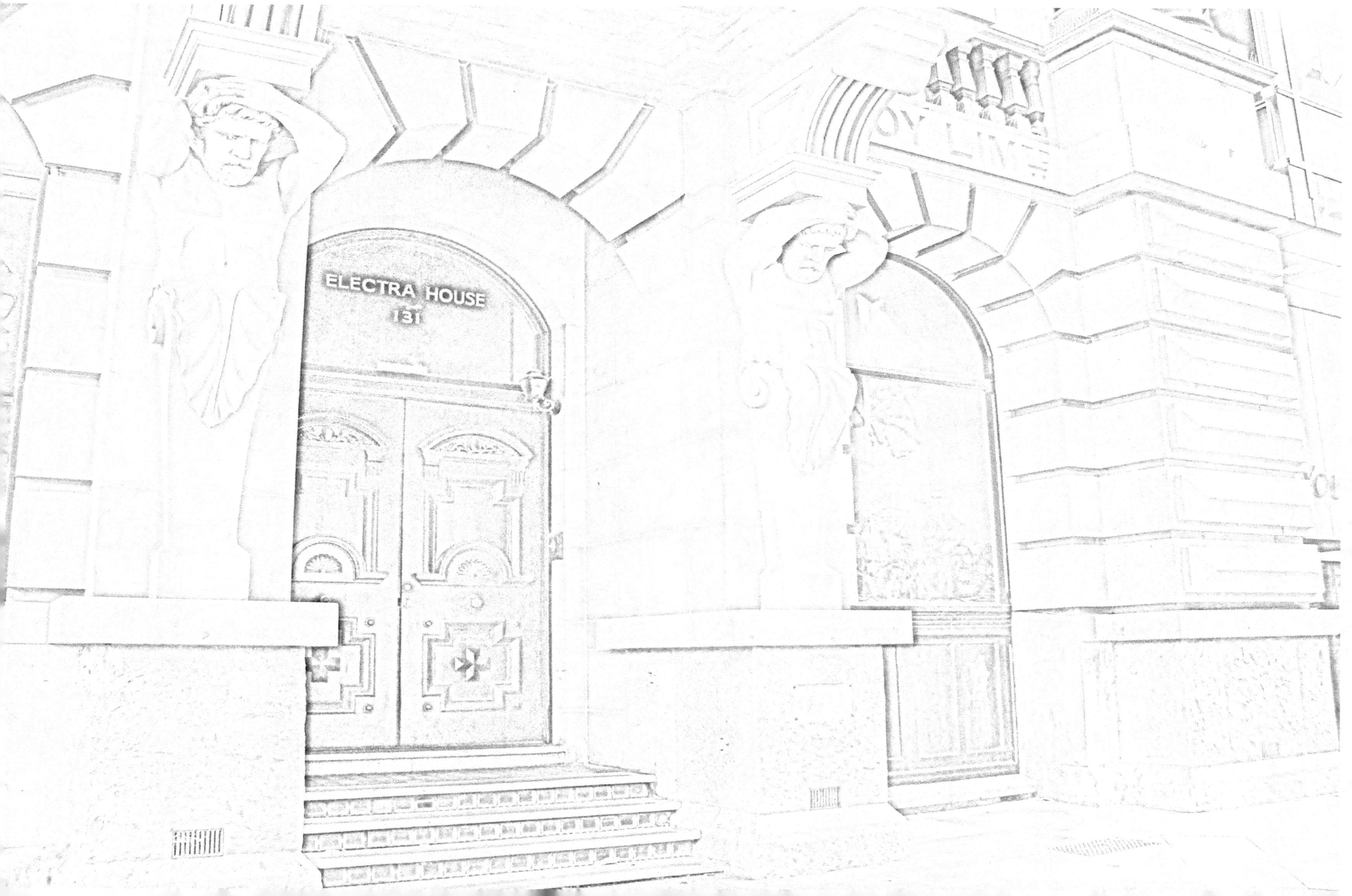
ELECTRA HOUSE
131

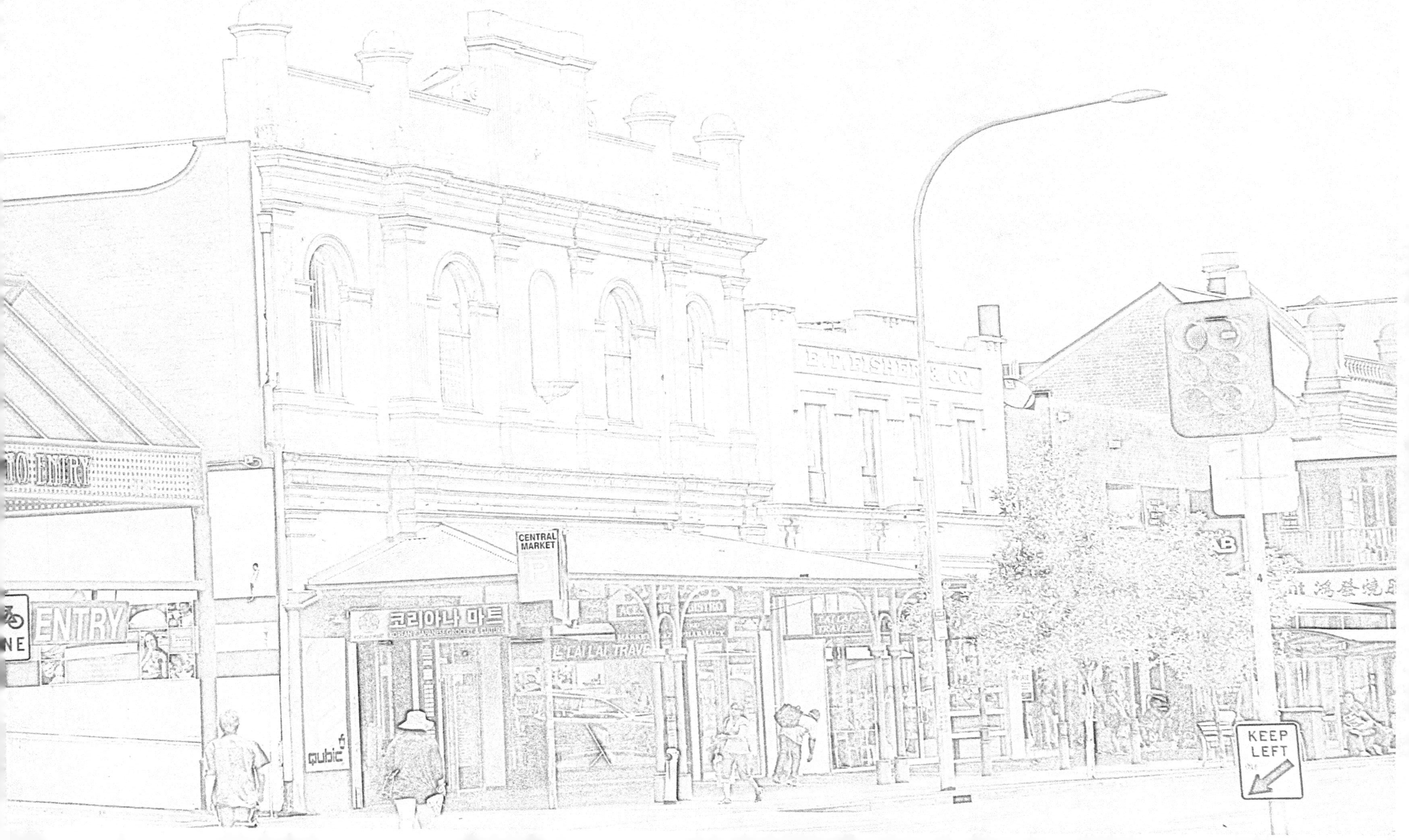

CENTRAL MARKET
코리아나 마트
ENTRY
qubic
KEEP LEFT

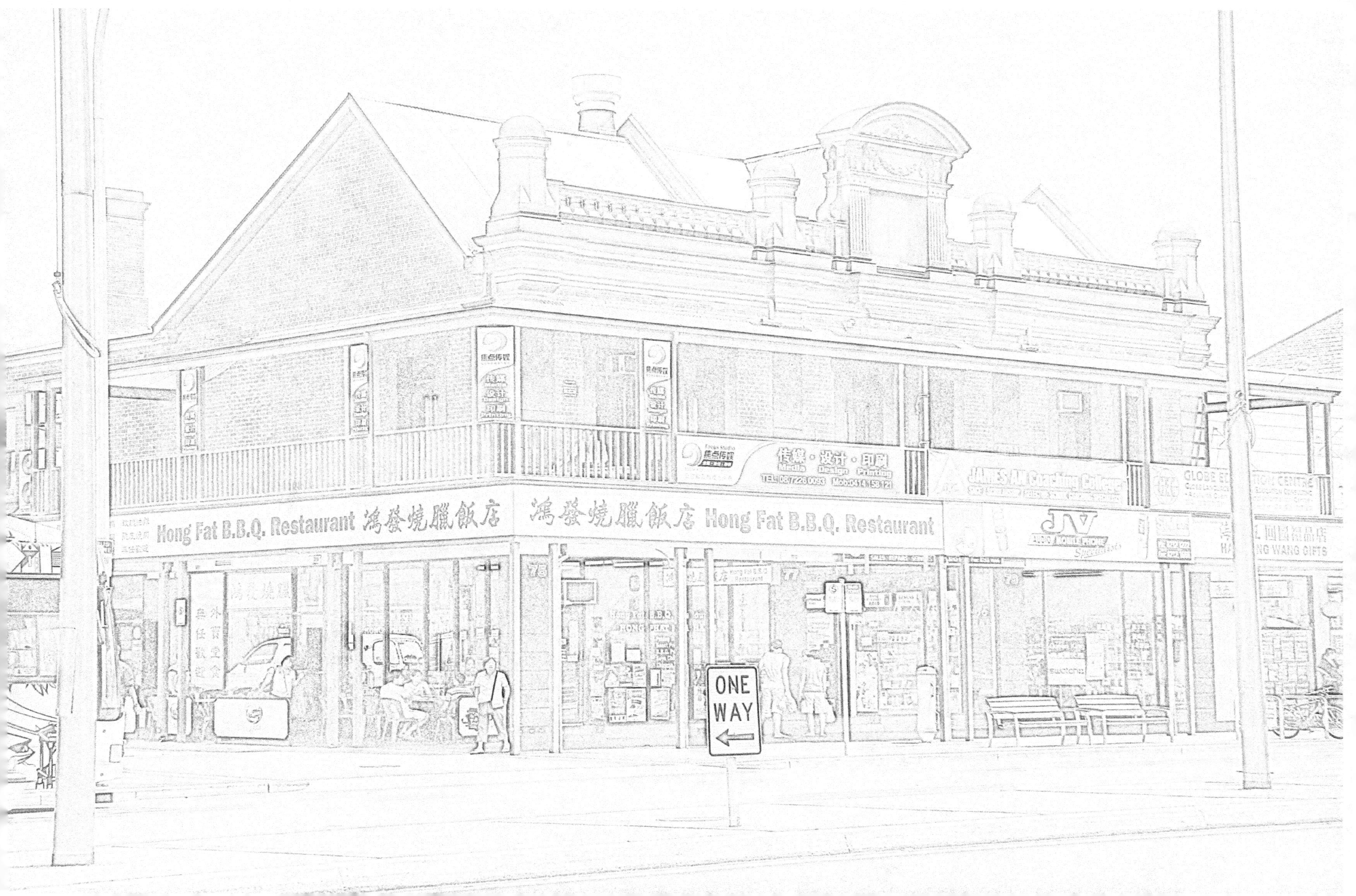
Hong Fat B.B.Q. Restaurant 鴻發燒臘飯店
鴻發燒臘飯店 Hong Fat B.B.Q. Restaurant
传媒・设计・印刷
Media Design Printing
ONE WAY
GLOBE ED
TION CENTRE
NG WANG GIFTS

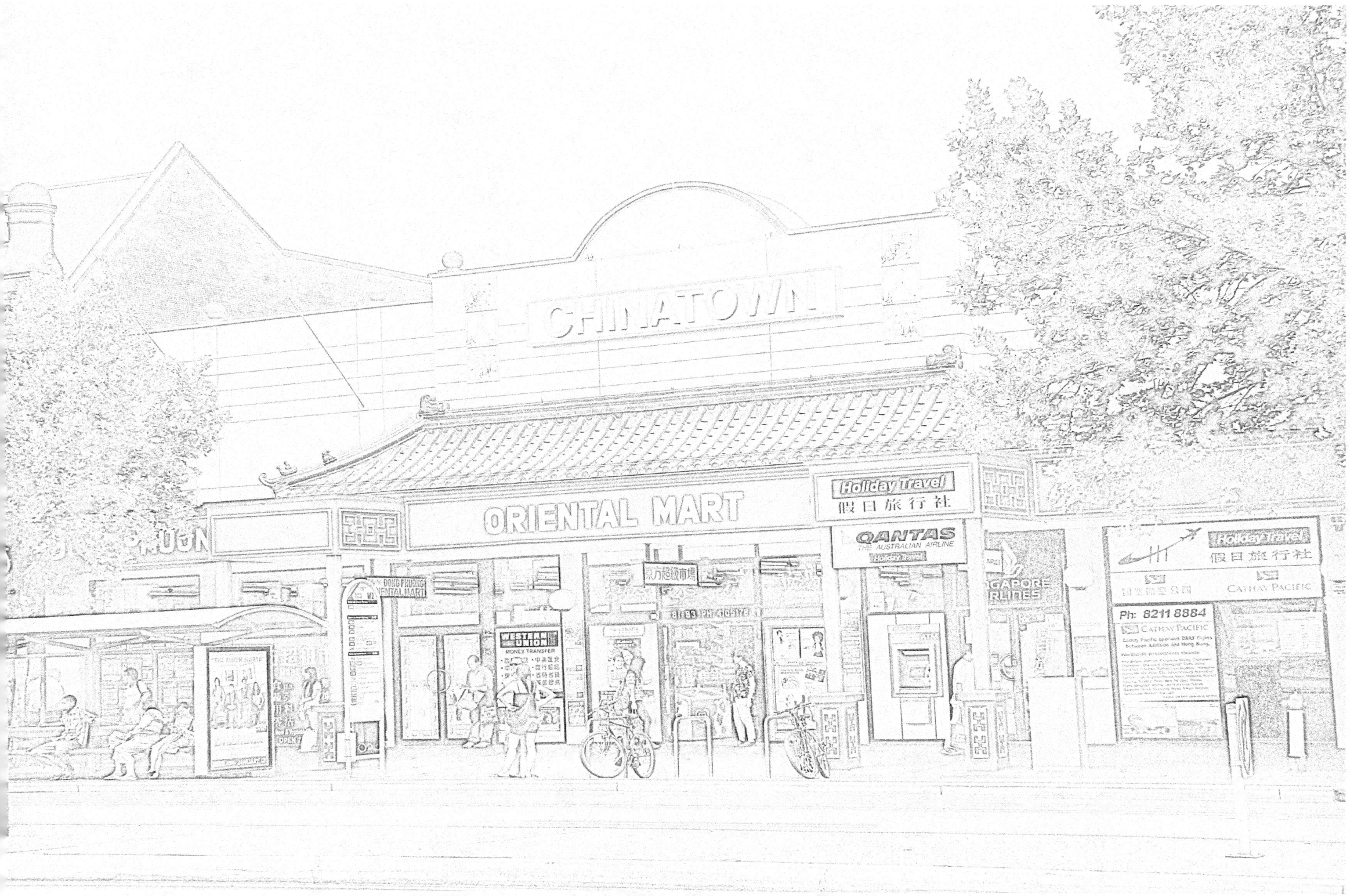
CHINATOWN
ORIENTAL MART
Holiday Travel
假日旅行社
QANTAS
THE AUSTRALIAN AIRLINE
Holiday Travel
Holiday Travel
假日旅行社
CATHAY PACIFIC
Ph: 8211 8884
CATHAY PACIFIC
WESTERN UNION
MONEY TRANSFER
DONG PHUONG
ORIENTAL MART
東方超級市場
GAPORE
RLINES

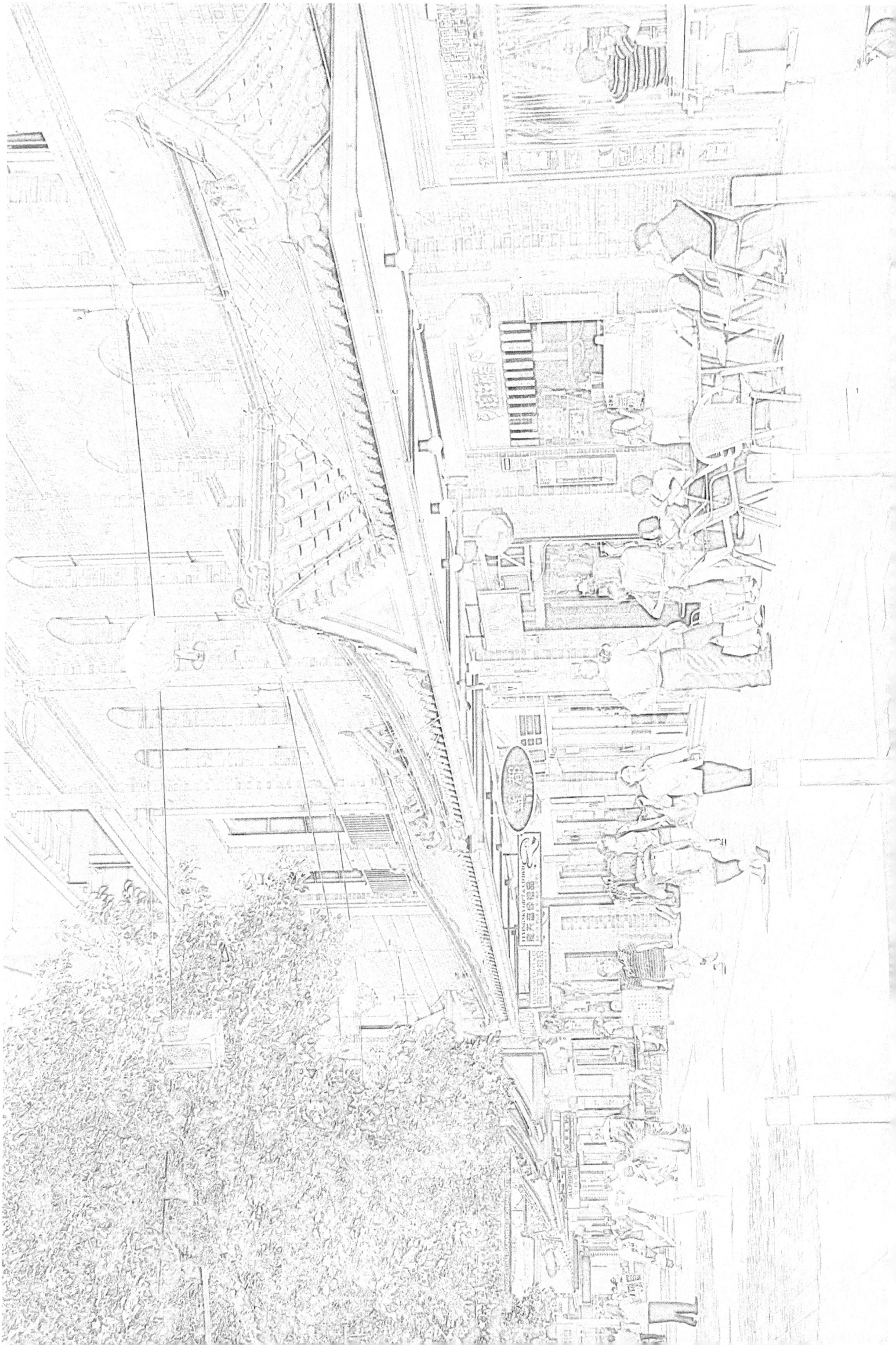

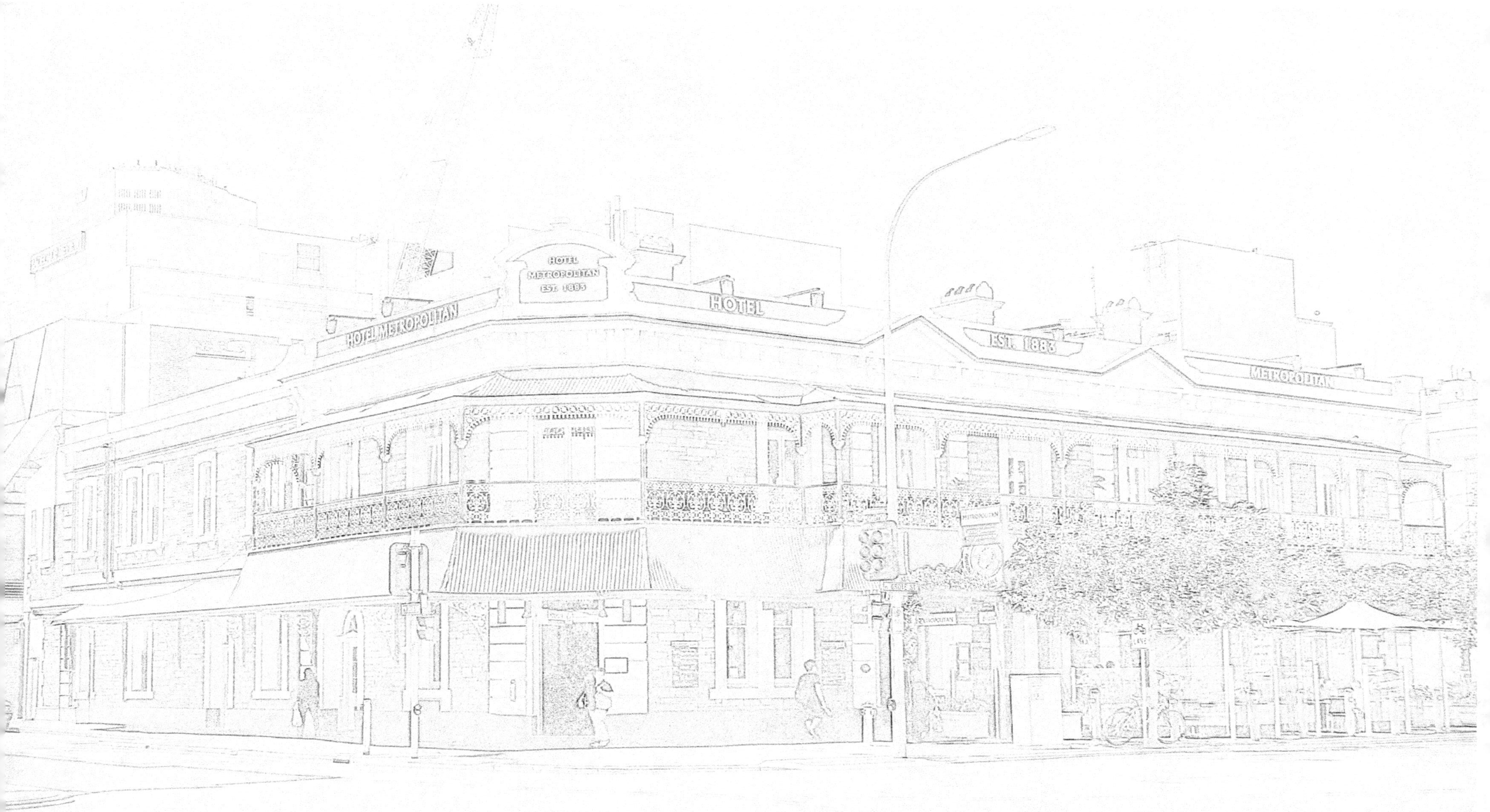

HOTEL
METROPOLITAN
EST. 1885
HOTEL METROPOLITAN
HOTEL
EST. 1883
METROPOLITAN

ISUZU

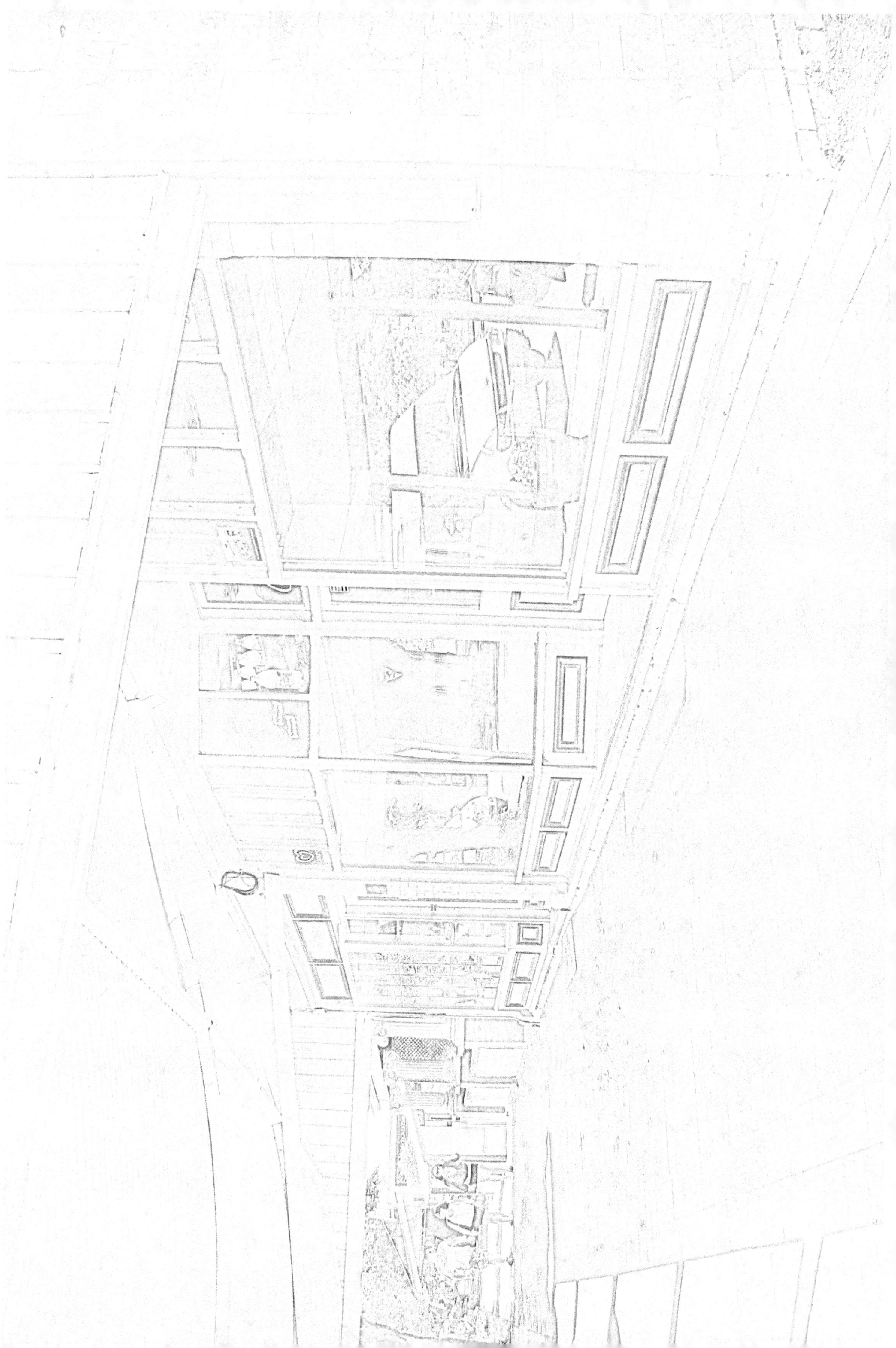

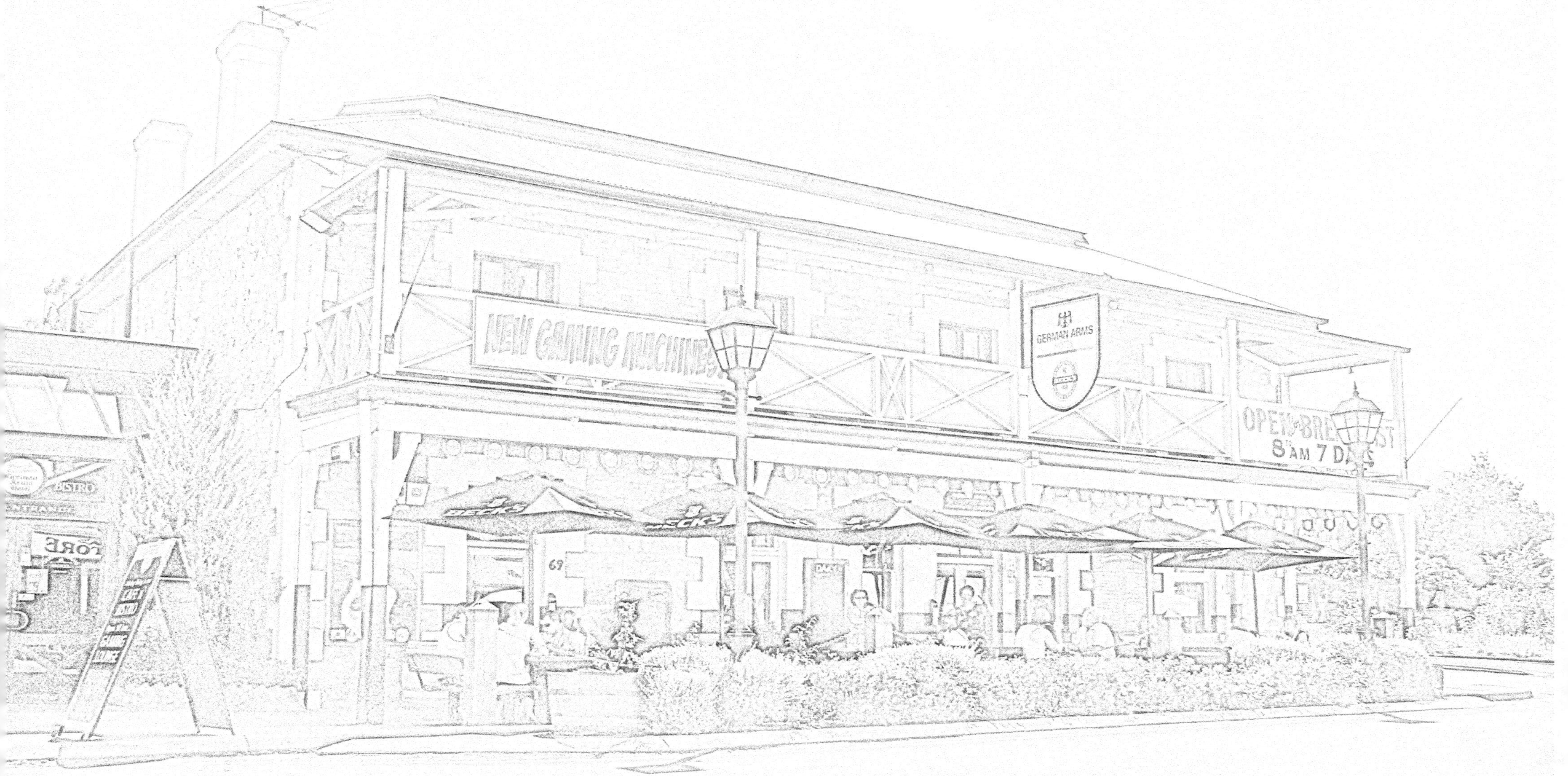
NEW GAMING MACHINES
GERMAN ARMS
BECKS
OPEN
8AM 7
BISTRO
69

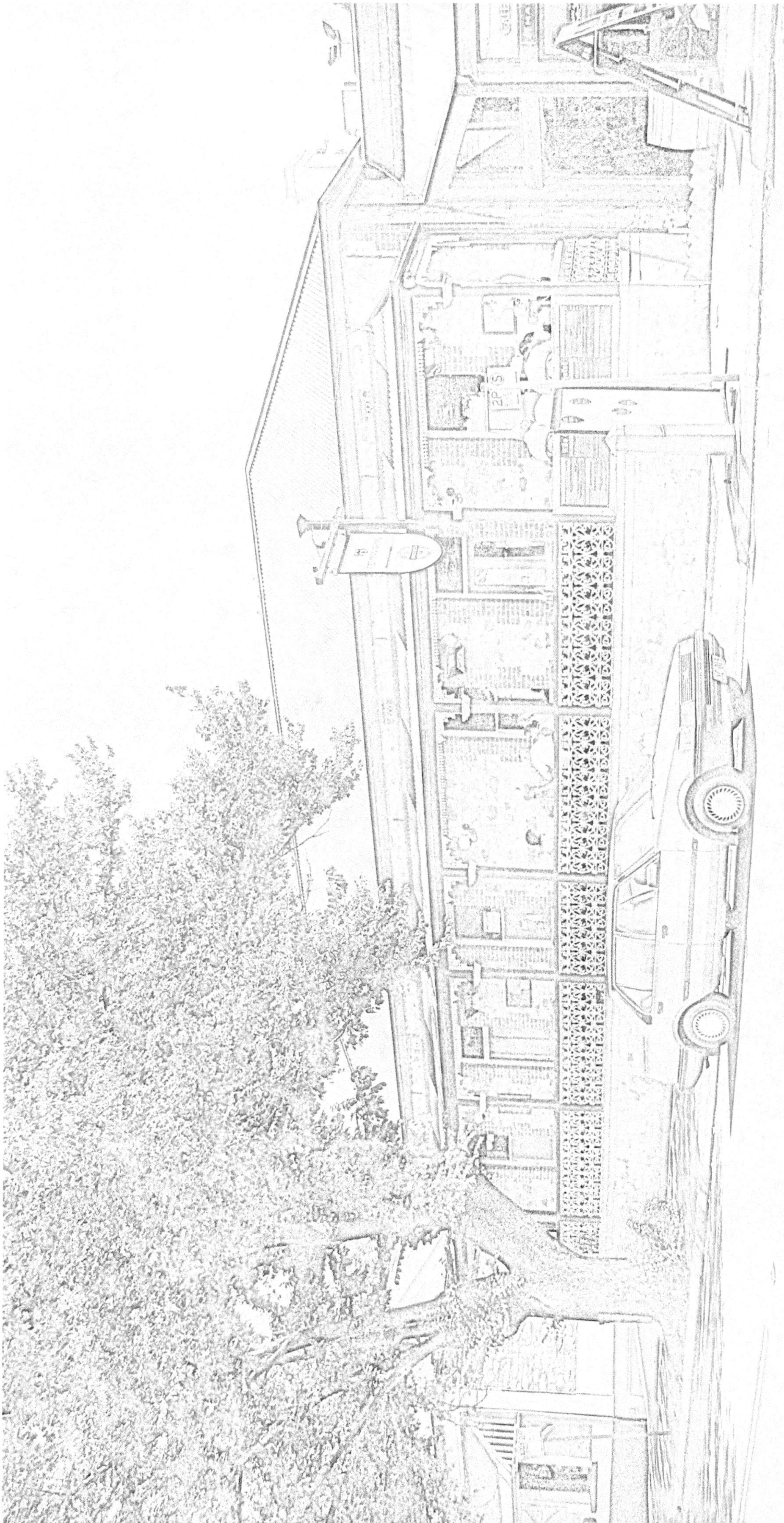

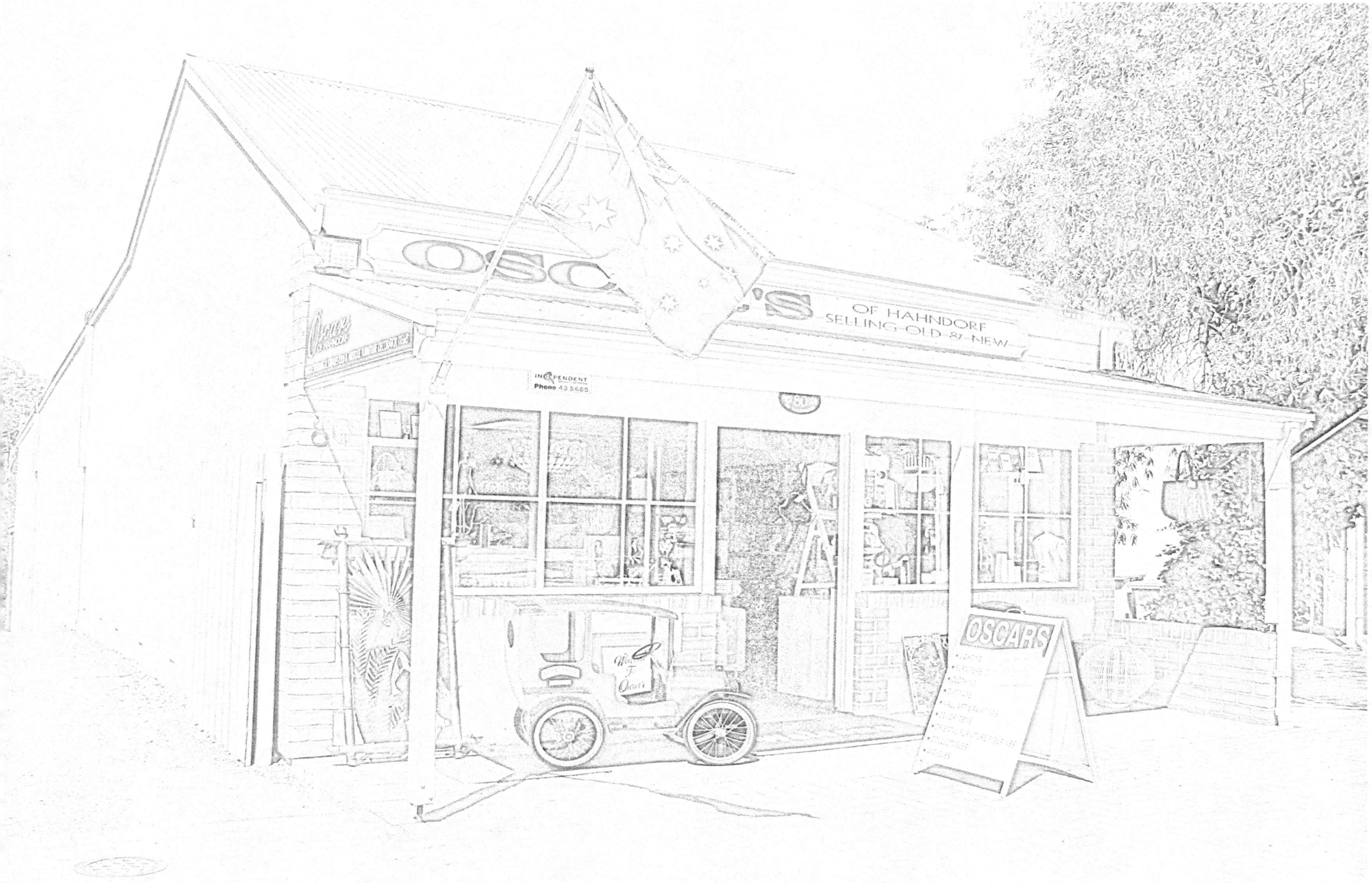
OF HAHNDORF
SELLING OLD & NEW
INDEPENDENT
Phone 43 5665
OSCARS

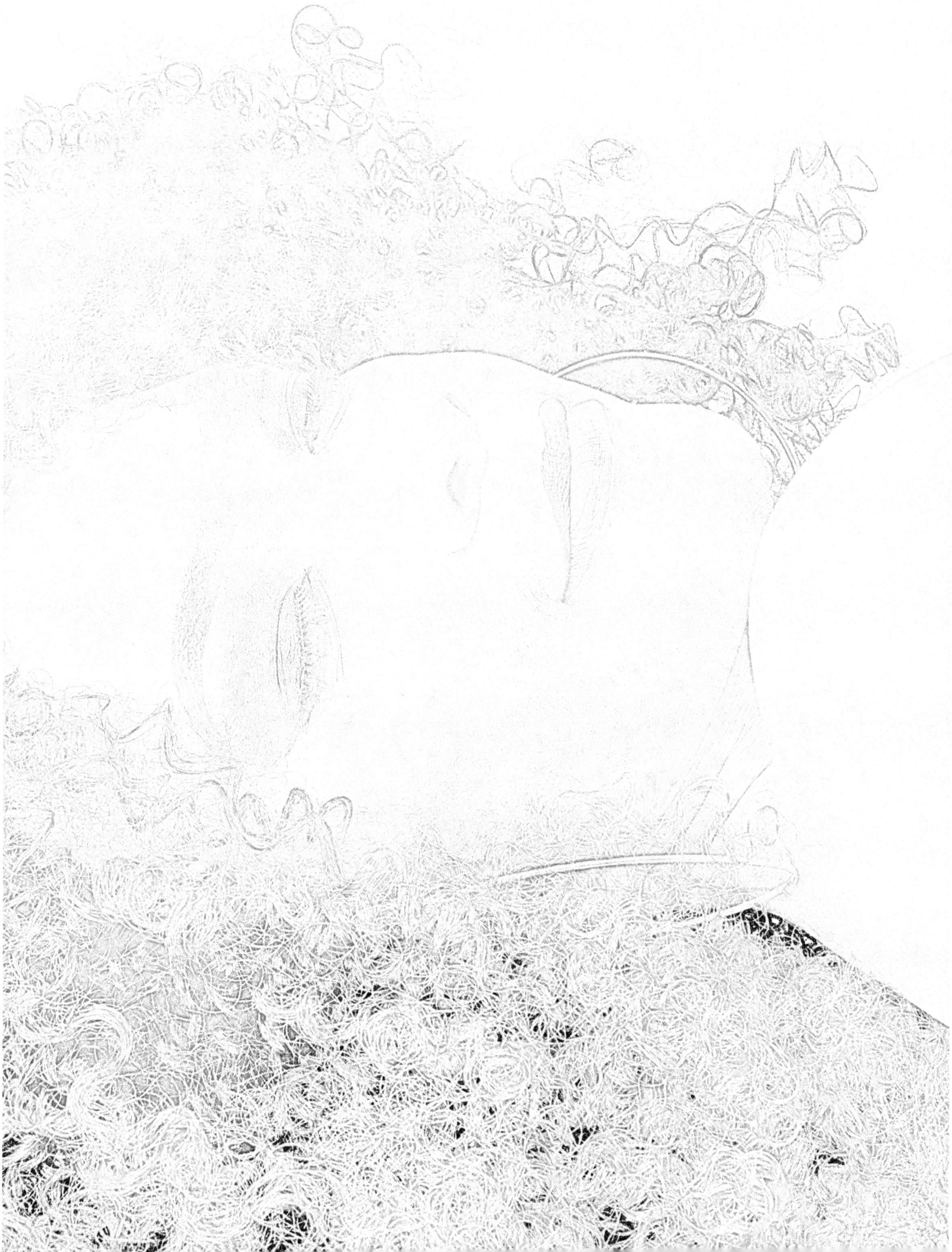

www.ingramcontent.com/pod-product-compliance
Lightning Source LLC
Chambersburg PA
CBHW081057180526
45170CB00005B/1795